Financial Aid and Beyond

SECRETS TO COLLEGE AFFORDABILITY

Updated Version June, 2016

Fred Amrein, MBA

The publication is designed to provide accurate educational information in regard to the subject matter covered in this book as of the date of this publication. The author and publisher are not offering it as legal, accounting, or other financial professional advice. Since tax laws, financial aid regulations, and government regulations change periodically, it is sold with the understanding that neither the publisher nor the authors are engaged in rendering legal, tax, investment or other professional services. If legal advice or other financial assistance is required the services of a competent professional person should be sought.

Although the author and publisher have made every effort to ensure that the information in this book was correct at press time, the author and publisher do not assume and hereby disclaim any liability to any party for any loss, damage, or disruption caused by errors or omissions, whether such errors or omissions result from negligence, accident, or any other cause. The advice and strategies contained herein may not be suitable for every situation.

CONTENTS

ACKNOWLEDGMENTS

I would like to thank and acknowledge everyone who helped me write this book. Without their contributions, this book would not have gotten written. First of all, I would like to thank my wife, Gerrie, who not only helped write this book but also reread countless editions before the final book was submitted. Her patience and direction were inspirational.

I am also grateful for my three daughters, who are my gifts from God. Friends who helped in the revisions and direction include Martha Bullen and Erin McHugh. My family and many others helped to form this project into the comprehensive book it became.

Finally, I would like to thank my clients and colleagues. You gave me the idea to write this book. I hope that it will provide college financial literacy to both parents and students, today and in the future.

Fred Amrein

OVERVIEW OF COLLEGE AFFORDABILITY

As a college-funding expert, I see the stress and fear that families experience when trying to choose the best college. While the value of a college education is obvious, the process of funding that education is anything but. In Financial Aid and Beyond, I will provide insights to guide you through the various decisions required over the course of the college-funding process.

Initially, students attempt to understand and evaluate various colleges' academic programs, cost of attendance, and social opportunities on campus. As students narrow their list of colleges, they begin to consider their competition and carefully look at their academic grades, standardized test scores, and involvement in extracurricular activities. Stress levels increase as students wait to receive acceptance letters and scholarships from their prospective colleges. Students and parents describe how overjoyed they are to receive acceptance letters from some or all of their top college choices. The next step is to commit not only to attending the college but also to providing the required financial resources for the degree.

With tuition and related college expenses increasing each year, effective college financing is more important than ever. This book addresses how financing decisions will affect your college affordability both today and after graduation. I will describe in detail the financial components involved in the Expected Family Contribution (EFC) and help students and their families understand their college award letters. It is my desire to help you make financial decisions that better advance your future and decrease the likelihood of making costly mistakes.

What Resources Are Available to Parents?

If you were making a $100,000 to $250,000 investment decision, would you seek professional help or a second opinion? I think most people would. In the case of the college investment decision, there is a significant amount of free advice available from the federal government, colleges and the internet. The financial aid process is even called the Free Application for Federal Student Aid. The same can be said about completing your taxes and the free advice available in that process. The IRS provides all the free information you need to complete your taxes, but most people do not complete their own taxes; they turn to either a professional or software for help.

As you go through the college selection process, keep in mind that a college education is a significant personal financial decision. It is also a business for the university. When making this personal financial decision, it is vital to get the right information from the correct source. The list below explains the sources of college information and provides a general overview of their expertise.

High School Guidance Counselors

This should be the first person you contact. High school guidance counselors know the students and their accomplishments. They have the greatest insights on which schools to apply to and the likelihood of a student being admitted. These professionals will know how prior students have fared at each college, and they have access to information from college admission officers that the public doesn't. The high school counselor's expertise is in the area of academic and campus fit.

Most high school counselors do not have a good knowledge of the financial aid process due to its complexity. Because of the specific personal financial information that needs to be disclosed, many high school counselors will minimize their involvement in the financial aid discussion.

The counselor or school will typically have a financial aid night and invite a local college financial aid officer to explain the financial aid process. These financial aid nights can only provide limited advice; their focus is the financial aid process and not the personal financial issues that this decision requires.

College Admission Counselors

If you look at the college education process as a business, college admission counselors are the salespeople. They will explain the benefits of their college or university with the primary goal of getting you to apply to their school.

Most admission counselors have limited knowledge of the financial aid process, but many colleges are trying to improve their admission staff's knowledge in this area, since college affordability is becoming an important part of the decision process.

Find out who the college representative is in your geographic area for each college that you are considering. The student should show interest in the college by attending the high school visit by the college representative, visiting the booth at a college fair, or making an actual visit to the school. Colleges are tracking this information more closely these days, and this could affect your admission chances.

The admission office can provide the initial information on the various scholarships or free money available at a college. It is important to understand that there are several variables involved in the free money given by a school.

Insider Note:

In this new world of electronic communication, colleges are beginning to track students' interest in their schools. Many colleges track in-person visits, e-mail responses, and other electronic interactions. This does not mean you should send an e-mail each day, but technology now allows college admission counselors to see your level of interest in their college. This recent change is becoming more sophisticated as we move to a more personal electronic form of marketing.

College Financial Aid Officers

College financial aid officers probably have the hardest job in the college decision process. These professionals provide the free financial advice from the college, but are limited to only the financial aid area. They work with the various college offices to help the institution meet the financial needs of the admitted and current students. This includes the deployment of federal, state and college funds.

The many regulations set by the federal and state governments make the financial aid process extremely regimented. They cannot provide a family with insights on how to maximize their financial resources with 529 plans, alternative financing options, or various tax strategies that can lower your out-of-pocket cost.

Some people assume that they can negotiate financial aid with the colleges. This is somewhat overstated. If you exclude the funds under the college's own control, changes in a financial award amount need to come with both documentation and sound reasons.

Why do families sometimes believe that there is more money available at the college of their choice? Some of the problem lies with the advertising of the colleges. Colleges often state in their marketing copy that they have plenty of financial aid. This encourages students to apply and sometimes creates false hope for both students and their families. In reality, the financial aid process is largely automated and follows specific rules, especially for the federal financial aid money. The customer gets an impression of affordability that may not really exist.

College financial aid officers handle many of the complaints and appeals for more money from families. This is a difficult job where expectations and emotions can be high. Treating these people with respect and having proper documentation can go a long way.

State Agencies

Most states have an agency that assists the general public with the college-funding process. These organizations can be very helpful, especially if your state has a higher education grant program. They will explain the grants available and provide information on federal financial aid programs.

These professionals are also limited to providing advice about the federal and state financial aid processes. They cannot provide detailed information on a specific college (like the college financial aid officer) or address personal financial issues that accompany the college affordability decision.

College Advisors

Due to the increased complexity of the college process and the growing importance of this decision, more families are using college planners. Another reason for this trend is the reduction of support staff at the high school level. As more and more students attend postsecondary programs, additional stress is placed on high school guidance counselors. Budget cuts have increased the student-to-counselor ratio, resulting in less time for each student and family to get the advice needed in the college decision process. This support level will vary by school.

College advisors offer a variety of services to help high school students gain admission to their selected colleges. These services vary greatly but usually include standardized testing preparation, essay editing, college list creation, college application assistance, scholarship search, and college best-fit search. Most college advisors offer programs at various price points.

HECA and IECA are two major college-planning organizations in the United States:

HECA   Higher Education Consultants Association
                    www.HECAonline.org
IECA   Independent Education Consultant Association
                    www.IECAonline.com

Members of these organizations are required to visit a certain number of colleges per year. They can provide personal insights from their expertise and networks that families may not have access to. Colleges now market to these groups.

The one shortfall of college planners is their limited knowledge of college-funding solutions. Most college advisors have a basic knowledge of the financial aid process but are limited in the financial advice they can provide due to legal requirements.

Financial Advisors

Financial advisors are not necessarily college-funding experts. To be college-funding experts, advisors need to have expertise in financial aid positioning, college saving plans, educational tax credits, student loans, and student-loan repayment. They also need a general understanding of the college admission process and personal financial issues such as retirement planning and portfolio design.

If you decide to employ a financial advisor to help create a college-funding strategy, you must do your research. It is a very specialized area. Actually, the financial service industry has gotten a bad reputation in the area of college financial aid because some financial advisors use the process to promote inappropriate financial product solutions.

Full disclosure of your financial information is necessary in order to calculate your financial aid position and your expected family contribution. Be careful—some financial aid advisors will use this opportunity to sell you other financial products. In my years of college financial planning, there have only been a few clients for whom life insurance or an annuity was an appropriate college-funding solution. It's important to understand both the short- and long-term impact of purchasing these financial products as part of your college-funding plan.

If you are looking for professional help in the financial area, I would suggest the website EFCplus.com. This excellent resource contains college-funding videos, a free EFC calculator, and current blog articles.

I am a charter and board member of the National College Advocacy Group (www.NCAGonline.org). In my opinion, this group provides its members with the best college financial information in the industry. There is a list of advisors to consider on the group's website.

> **Insider Note:**
>
> Be very careful of financial advisors who promote annuity and life insurance products as college-funding solutions. In most cases, these solutions are not appropriate for long-term college planning. Instead, I recommend working with a financial advisor who is a fiduciary. Fiduciaries are financial advisors who must act in their clients' best interests. They must also disclose all compensation if asked.

The Admission Focus

For many students, the focus of the college decision is limited to the admission process and school selection. Students' application strengths will vary depending on the size and type of college they are considering.

The two major areas that schools review are the quantifiable information and the subjective data. Each college will weigh these differently. Below are the major items they consider:

Quantifiable data:
- Current academic grades or GPA

- Standardized testing (SAT or ACT)

- Academic course selection (both course and academic difficulty level)

- Class ranking

- High school academic quality rating (some colleges rate the academic strength of each high school)

- Family's financial position

Subjective data:
- Leadership qualities or experience

- Essay

- Activities

- Reference letters

- First-generation college applicant

- Race

- Sex

- State residence

- Special skills

- Interest in the college

- Application Method

- Specific program/major application

- Social media image

The colleges spend a great deal of effort trying to create the desired mix of students that they want in their admitted class. Schools have sophisticated modeling and marketing tools to track their admitted and plan to attend students. With the use of computer technology and the speed of information, schools are very good at projecting their desired class outcomes. This admission data is monitored very closely, similar to any good business tracking their projected sales.

It is important to realize that admission does not mean affordable. Students and parents often confuse this due to the way schools market their programs.

An Emotional Period

The college decision process can be emotional and stressful for both parents and students. Listed below are a series of questions repeated by many of my clients as they've gone through the college decision process:

- What schools should I apply to and why?

- Should I consider a two-year community school, trade school, or four-year college?

- How can I decide on a major and possible career?

- Should I apply for early decision, early action, or regular decision?

- What are the deadlines for applications and financial aid forms?

- How do I learn more about financial aid, scholarships, and student loans?

- What do the award letters mean, and how can we get more money?

Students and parents face these decisions as they navigate through the college decision process. For parents going through this for the first time, it can be even more worrisome and confusing, but being patient and organized can minimize the stress inherent in this process.

One of the biggest mistakes families make is focusing on being admitted to a particular school and not on the desired educational outcome. In the emotional high of being admitted to a highly selective or dream school, students and parents sometimes, minimize the importance of choosing an effective educational path. A critical factor is allotting the financial resources needed to reach the desired academic and financial results. Here is where the system needs to change.

As college costs continue to rise and employment opportunities become more competitive, having a focus on the overall educational outcome is critical. The successful college experience requires the proper mix of networking, academics, career planning and graduating on time to be positive. This puts additional pressure on the student and family. The actual cost of an additional year of college and the opportunity cost of not working are significant. This is a very different environment than most parents faced during their college experience.

Ideally, students should select their major by the end of their first year or at least feel comfortable that they are on track with their current academic major decision. Students should take ownership of their progress toward that goal. While colleges have a stake in students' success and make resources available to them, the problem is that each school will engage students differently. Students may overlook these resources, especially early on.

Parents should be involved during this time but need to become more of a mentor. Your child will also need to take ownership of this freedom and responsibility. The college expects the student to take full responsibility of the process. I believe it is a time of transition for the student and parent relationship. Both the student and parent need to communicate their objectives of a college education.

Minimize the stress by having open discussions early on and by talking with your child about what the family can afford. The plan should be flexible and include an educational goal for the next four years, combining both the academic possibilities and the affordability of the college. The EFCplus website (www.EFCplus.com) and this book will help you develop that plan.

> **Insider Note:**
>
> According to the 2013 Digest of Education Statistics, only 39 percent of college students pursuing a bachelor degree graduate in four years. This increases to 54.9 percent in five years and 58.7 percent in six years. These are averages for all college types that include public, non-profit and for profit institutions.

Understanding the Application Numbers

The increased number of people attending college has changed the admission process. In 2011, according to *Digest of Education Statistics*, the number of enrolled students aged eighteen to twenty-four reached 42 million. Let us compare that to 1985, when that same group totaled 27.8 million students. This is an increase of over 51 percent, and that does not include older students who have returned to college for a variety of reasons. The most recent numbers are from 2012 and show that over 41 million students were then enrolled in postsecondary education.[1]

As with most businesses, supply and demand dictates pricing changes in college fees. This is one of the reasons why college costs have risen at the rate they have. With growing attendance rates, colleges built new buildings to accommodate the additional students.

As the demand for students has increased, so has competition among colleges. As new buildings are built and amenities enhanced, students and parents develop higher expectations of what a college campus should deliver from an environmental standpoint. Keeping pace with students' expectations becomes a vicious circle for colleges.

The competition to attract the best students to fit the schools' profiles is great. Most parents did not face this situation when making their college decision because at that time there were fewer college-bound students and a growing demand for college-educated professionals. Our children face a different environment: increased college admissions competition, more college-educated people available, and a job market that is flat.

Test-Optional Colleges

Students often find it stressful to take the various standardized tests usually required for college admission, such as the SAT or ACT exams. Most students take these tests two or three times. However, over the past few years, more colleges are beginning to make the test scores optional as part of their admission process.

Schools are starting to realize that students' academic ability and success can be represented more accurately in their current grades rather than by a one-day test. With the new option available, college-bound students will need to put more focus on their academic grades and course selection. This will only be a slight change, since grades have always been important.

I do not see standardized testing going away. For merit-based scholarships, it will still be needed.

Insider Note:

The test-score-optional colleges are listed on www.fairtest. org.

Now that you have some of the background and landscape of the area of college funding, we will move on to the specifics of creating a plan and making the best college decision. The best college decision will focus on the outcome of the education. The best college decision will factor the financial, academic, and environmental aspects of each college.

ADMISSIONS DOES NOT MEAN AFFORDABILITY

In this chapter, I will explain how most colleges filter their admission and financial aid decisions; this information is not always fully disclosed to students or their families. As I stated in the first chapter, colleges are businesses; they do not make decisions based on emotion and nor should you. As much as possible, try to remove emotion from the college decision; this will make it easier to be objective as you move through the various stages of the process. If you take a value approach to your college decision, the outcome will more likely be favorable.

Process Evolution

The college decision process has become more complicated for both students and parents as technology and transportation have increased our ability to investigate a wider variety of colleges. The broader options make it more difficult to narrow the selection. Parents and students are also able to get more information on how the process works. At times, the amount of data can become overwhelming.

The college admission process is no different. On the student side, we first had the standardized testing prep programs, then essay editors, and now college coaches. The colleges have evolved too. They added essays to the application process, the standardized tests have changed, and the use of social media is becoming more important. However, the biggest change in recent years has been the evolution of the enrollment management office. At most colleges, this department manages and coordinates the activities of both the admissions and financial aid offices. Depending on the institution, the enrollment management group can have a significant impact on other activities and departments at the college. This will vary from college to college.

Due to the increased financial demands and expectations of college students, colleges needed to become more organized and operate more like businesses. With college enrollment up over 47.8 percent since 1985,[2] colleges need to be more competitive to attract the best students. Just as in any other thriving business, understanding the basics of supply and demand is critical.

Because of this new environment, colleges have created sophisticated marketing, admissions, selection, and revenue models as part of the enrollment management process. This process varies by college with each school determining its own specific goals. The problem is that the public is unaware of how complex this process really is and how it really works. From a marketing standpoint, the colleges communicate a level of simplicity to the families. In reality, the process is much more sophisticated than families realize.

Law of Large Numbers

In a recent seminar with various experts in the enrollment management area, a dominant point of conversation was the colleges' goal of increasing the number of college applications each year. By increasing the amount of applications, colleges are better able to reach their projected admission target goals. As with any business, increasing the customer base is important.

Here a few reasons colleges promote application submissions:

- Improves their selectivity ratings for the national publications

- Increases their ability to create the ideal class profile

- Income from paid applications reduces admissions operating cost

- Greater ability to reach target revenue through larger application mix

If you were starting a new business or organization, would you like to have the option to select from a larger or smaller pool of possible employees? The law of large numbers will normally work in your favor and provide a better overall outcome.

Let us invert the process for a minute. When students start their college lists, they have thousands of schools that can be on their college list. Colleges do the same thing. They try to create the greatest amount of interest possible so that they can select from the best pool of applicants.

Most students have experienced the law of large numbers as part of a selection process; the problem is that many just did not realize it at the time. As students grow up, they face increased competition at the things they try, such as sports or music. Depending on their abilities and maybe a little luck, some students will continue to be successful. Others will be forced out by the competition and need to find an alternative to their abilities.

Depending on the student's college list, this may be the first time he or she is competing at a national level.

The Student's Perspective

Creating a list of potential colleges can be a difficult task. It may provide a taste of reality based on the student's academic progress. Some of the students were hopeful about gaining admission to various colleges but are no longer in the running due to a variety of reasons. It is best to keep an open mind at the beginning of this process and evaluate all of the options.

Having good grades can also sometimes create an expectation for students that they will be admitted into all of their selected colleges.

However, good grades are only one piece of the puzzle. A family's ability to pay or the diversity you bring to that school is also very important.

One of the most common starting points for college-bound students is an academic scattergram. Software programs that can help you create academic scattergrams are available at most high schools. I would recommend that you contact your school's college guidance office to see what is available.

The scattergram will show how you compare to other students admitted to the college in question. This can be a very helpful filtering tool. These charts do not display that a lower GPA student took a more difficult curriculum or that he or she was a class president. The academic strength of a student is just one aspect of determining the probability of admission.

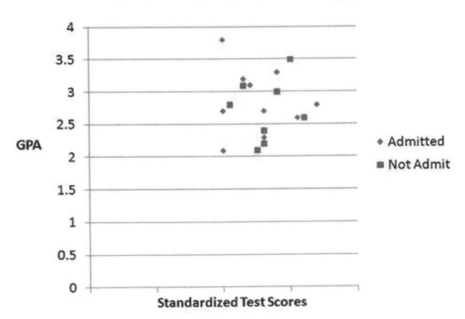

Please note that the scattergram above is purely a plotting of academic information, but the admission decision will include other factors beyond academics. In the above example, based on the students admitted, this college seems to place more emphasis on grade point average (GPA) than standardized test scores. The high school guidance counselors or college advisors normally know these insights.

The data points reveal that the student with the second-lowest GPA was accepted. This student may have a unique talent or skill that the college wants to have as part of its entering freshman class.

This chart can give you an idea of how you stand in just one aspect of the college admission process. There are many other factors that are not shown on this chart, such as teacher recommendations, difficulty of classes, whether you're applying as a first-generation college student, and which state you live in, just to name a few.

Many families only evaluate the likelihood of the student being accepted into a college based on academics. Some students and parent will begin to evaluate the other areas each college may be looking for, especially in athletics, performing arts or a specific major. This is an important step. The problem with this approach is that it creates a silo effect on the decision process.

Decision Analysis

| Academic | Demographic | Special Skills | Environment | Financial Aid |

Using a silo approach makes it hard for students to quantify where they are in comparison to other applicants. Here is where the colleges have an advantage; they use very sophisticated selection tools to consider all of these factors simultaneously in order to create their desired entering class. These tools can also project future revenue generated by their selection decision.

Plotting as many factors in the admission process as possible is key to evaluating a student's probability of admission and affordability. The key word here is *affordability*. Being admitted to any college is an accomplishment, but the ability to attend normally comes down to finances. Colleges have the greatest advantage in this area. They can make the financial award package unattractive, resulting in less-well-off students not being able to attend.

The College Decision Matrix

We have all heard the stories of child X being accepted to a college and receiving a certain amount of scholarship. Both students and parents tend to generalize many issues regarding the college selection process. This can cloud the true picture and not reflect the true outcome of the admission process. People do not realize the amount of analysis a college will use in their selection decisions. Simple variances can make a significant difference in admissions and certain financial awards.

Some colleges use the free money terminology to confuse an issue or make the student feel good. For example, some scholarships are based on need while others are based on merit. You may have two admitted students that both receive a listed scholarship on their award letter. In reality, both could have very different academic and admission profiles. One may have received money for merit reasons, such as high grades, and the other received the money for need-based reasons. While both students received scholarship money from the college, in this case, the scholarship money was awarded for very different reasons. Most people will only hear the term *scholarship*. This is an example of how myths develop in the college admissions and financial aid process.

As mentioned earlier, this is where colleges bring together the law of large numbers and selecting the best applicants. Each school has a specific desired class profile that will generate the revenue it needs. Even though the admission process has significant subjectivity, the college will quantify many elements to minimize its risk of adverse selection.

Once the college has quantified the student, it places each applicant into a bucket within an admission-potential grid. This grid is similar to the scattergram shown above but uses only the current year's applicant pool. The history of the past applicant pool will be used to help classify each student. Depending on the college, a group of individuals will rank each person within the buckets to complete the school's class profile.

Since the application process normally precedes the financial aid process, some colleges will use the financial aid process to enhance or deter students from attending their college. This is especially true when students need financial aid to attend a college. A student's application method may have an impact on the amount of financial aid received and this should be considered. To be accepted into college is one thing; to be able to afford it is another.

If the student will be applying to a college that offers early decision, a separate financial aid form is often required. The most common is the College Scholarship Service (CSS) Profile managed by College Board. Since early decision is binding, the only way to not accept early decision admittance is to state financial reasons. If you decline early decision, you can no longer attend that college in the upcoming year. As a general statement, early decision financial awards are normally less generous. Here is where weighing admission versus affordability options are important.

The CSS Profile is another financial aid process that is used by some colleges and scholarships. It is available in October. Due to the Prior Prior Department of Education change, the federal process called the Free Application for Federal Student Aid (FAFSA) will now be available on October 1, of each year. If you are applying early decision and financial aid is needed to attend that college, you will have to submit the CSS Profile. You will also need to complete the FAFSA, since this information will verify the CSS Profile information and is required for the federal financial aid programs.

> **Insider Note:**
>
> **Only sixty-one colleges in the United States (about 2 percent) meet 100 percent of financial need.** [3]

Once the financial information is available, the college can complete the selection process. Instead of envisioning the process in silos, most colleges use a matrix system. The level of admission attractiveness resides on the Y-axis and the student's financial need falls on the X-axis. (See the chart below.)

College Academic & Financial Aid Position

Sample College Info

Avg SAT	1150
Avg ACT	25
Avg GPA	3.50
Avg Financial Award	$16,000

Current Student
(Dot is Charted Student)

SAT	1250
ACT	28
GPA	3.65
Need	$19,500

EFC PLUS Sample Matrix

Academic

Q1   Q2

Q3   Q4

$ Financial Need
0 4 8 12 16 20 24 28 32 36 40

In the example above, you can see where the average academic position and the average financial aid package are for that college. The dot marks where this specific student rates at this specific college. A student's position will vary at each college based on the student's academic strength and the family's financial need. Most applicants are plotted on the grid to help the enrollment management group better project the class profile and potential revenue stream of the admitted students.

This is a sample of how colleges bring together the academic strength and needed financial aid for each student. In the chart above, there are four different quadrants. (These are very different from the EFC quadrants that I describe in the next chapter.) These quadrants are how colleges qualify each student's position for admission and financial aid. The sizes of each quadrant will vary by college.

Quadrant 1 (Q1): Students in this quadrant are above the average academic grades of the college and need less than the average financial aid package granted by the school.

Quadrant 2 (Q2): Students in this quadrant are above the average academic grades of the college and need more than the average financial aid package granted by the school.

Quadrant 3 (Q3): Students in this quadrant are below the average academic grades of the college and need less than the average financial aid package granted by the school.

Quadrant 4 (Q4): Students in this quadrant are below the average academic grades of the college and need more than the average financial aid package granted by the school.

Within the matrix, you will normally not move on the X-axis, or financial need chart, since this is based on your financial aid forms. However, there can be great movement on the Y-axis, since this graph only displays the student's academic position and not the other subjective factors that are analyzed. The Y-axis is really your admission strength at that college. It is important to realize that these are averages and each student is reviewed separately.

All the personal measures are added or subtracted to the academic side of the chart (Y-axis). I have mentioned the different variables colleges use to evaluate each student. Each college will weigh the variables differently. As an example, one college may put more weight on the quality of a student's course selection than standardized test scores. This is where making college visits, asking your high school counselor, and working with a college advisor may help you better understand the specific criteria each school uses in its selection process. These insights can help students improve their chances of being admitted to their preferred schools.

Seeing where you are on the chart is only a starting point. It will help you build your college list. It shows you the probability of your acceptance and affordability in the same graph. You need to remember that the admission decision has many subjective factors that may change each year for a college. This matrix is only a guide to the admission and financial award letter process.

With this chart, you are now starting to see how sophisticated this process is from the college standpoint. In fact, some schools use over three hundred buckets to rate their applicants in order to create the desired entering class and minimize the risk of revenue shortfalls. Colleges track this process very closely. During the application process, if the number of applications are down, additional resources will be directed to increase applications. During the acceptance period, detailed tracking of class profile and future revenue are managed on a daily basis.

Colleges try to predict the number of students that will accept the admission and award letter. This is called the college's admission yield, and it varies from year to year (with the exception of a few elite schools). Colleges do have some risks during this process, since enrollment does change each year. To minimize this risk, they use a historical yield to help project their results.

Colleges manage admission risk by using various other tools, including putting students on a wait list and attracting more students by offering additional financial aid during the decision period. The month of April is the normal decision time for most students. This could be changing due to the change in the FAFSA submission date moving to October and colleges having the information earlier.

These annual adjustments are a perfect example of how the myths, and sometimes the media, create a story about being able to negotiate with colleges. Some colleges will match competitors' financial aid offers, but in some cases, the additional financial award money may be simple luck. In a given year, a college may have a bad enrollment mix. It may try to attract a certain type of student with a higher net pay by providing some additional money. Here is where a simple inquiry may get a family some additional money. In other years, that same request would be denied.

As you can see, college admission is presented as a simple process, yet behind the scenes, it is very complex. Now that you have a better insight into how and why colleges admit potential students, this may change your application approach to each school.

Insider Note:

The college financial-planning software called EFC PLUS, provides an academic and financial aid matrix. It will help family's better understand their personal college affordability position at each college.

The New Reach View

Most everyone is familiar with the term "reach school." The student's academic strength is in the acceptable range but the student is border line for admission to certain schools. Considering the amount of subjectivity in the admission process, students should have a few reach schools on their college list. To improve your chances of admission at your reach schools, you will need to have a unique or special trait that the school may be looking for in the entering class. A college planner or your high school guidance office could be helpful with identifying these schools based on your individual skill set. Remember, the colleges are taking a holistic approach to their admission. A special talent or uniqueness is just one piece of the whole.

Not often discussed is the financial reach of a college. Many families look only at the sticker price and make their application decision with just that information. Others hear colleges marketing their abundance of financial aid funding and apply hoping they will get what they need to attend. Both of these situations can be mistakes for different reasons. This is why the college matrix can be so helpful when going through your application decisions.

One of my major reasons for writing this book is to provide an approach to the college application and decision process that will allow you to make a better choice. The EFC PLUS Matrix displays your personal position on both spectrums, academic and financial. This will show you how much reach you have in both areas of the admission process. Using this approach will give you a better understanding of your reach schools.

Ability to Pay

Part of the complexity of the admission process involves a deeper evaluation of a family's ability to pay college tuition. This pressure comes from a variety of places but mostly from the federal government. Unlike in previous years, colleges are now being held more accountable for their students' loan default rate.

I have noticed a new trend whereby parents are becoming more cost-conscious in the college selection process. Many have begun to limit their options based on the sticker price of the school, resulting in a significant increase in the quality and quantity of students attending state universities and the increased difficulty of getting into these lower-priced schools compared to past years.

Limiting your options based on sticker price can be a mistake. As I discussed earlier, colleges are looking to create a specific class profile. There are factors that can affect the admissions or the financial aid of a college. This can vary depending on the admission year. Schools could be focusing on a specific college major, SAT score, high school course selection, high school attended, race, gender or even the state residence. For example, if one year the enrollment is down in a Business major, the next year a college may increase the admission pool and bump up the scholarship award amount for that major. With these variables, it is sometimes

26

difficult to predict the application outcome for a family. It is where a higher priced college may become more affordable. Families should be looking for the best value, and that may not be the lowest price.

Another big problem with the college selection process is that schools only provide information one year at a time. College is normally a four-year financial commitment. To understand the true value of your college decision, you need to analyze the financials on a four-year basis. In the chapter "Paying for College," I will discuss the proper ways to plan for paying for college. The college affordability software, EFC PLUS allows you to do this by school based on your personal budget.

The EFC PLUS software projects the financial outcome or value of each college. Depending on when various children attend college and the colleges they select, the more expensive college can be price competitive over the four years. As consumers, parents should always look at the college value and not just the sticker price. Factoring in graduation rates, retention, and class size can make the higher-priced schools a better value proposition in different situations.

Better Application Decisions

With this new information from the matrix, I hope more families will be able to reduce the number of applications they submit. Under the current system, students have no idea where they are in the application and financial aid pool. This new perspective will give students and parents a better insight into how colleges perceive their admission probability in order to help them identify colleges where they will be a better academic and financial fit.

Applying to colleges has become increasingly expensive. Application costs can range from $40 to $100 per college, including the application fee, test score request, and high school transcript fees. Understanding what constitutes a "good fit" and what the net costs are important facts to be considered. With this data, parents and students are more informed consumers. It may help you reduce the number of colleges that the student applies to and save hundreds of dollars in application fees.

Application Methods

Before going into more detail on the financial aid aspect of the application process, I feel that a quick explanation of the different application methods needs to be described. Students and parents have the added complexity of trying to understand the meaning of early action, early decision, regular decision, and rolling admission. Each of these application methods have both admission and financial aspects to consider.

The decision to apply early decision is the most difficult since it is the most restrictive of the methods. With an early decision application, the student will apply to a college early and receive a decision typically by December of their senior year. If accepted under the early decision application, the student will enter into a binding agreement with that college to enroll. The student also will agree to withdraw all other applications and not accept any other offers of admission. Some schools are now offering two early decision options. Proper planning and deadline management is essential.

The one risk with using the early decision application process is the lack of ability to compare financial awards from different colleges. Since the student will not be applying to other schools, the net cost comparison of the other colleges will not be available. Due to restrictive nature of early decision, you need to feel comfortable that this is the only school you want to attend.

Some colleges also have the early action program in their admission process. The timing and process is similar to the early decision application yet the decision is not binding. If accepted under the early action method, the student can continue to apply to other colleges. The final college decision is not required until all of the admission letters have been received.

Most colleges that offer early decision and early action require a preliminary financial aid form. The most common is the CSS Profile. This CSS Profile financial aid process is more complex than the Federal Methodology or FAFSA. It is available in October. Check your application and financial form deadlines depending on the application method you decide to use. The early decision process may be changing due to

FAFSA timing change. You will need to confirm the financial forms needed and the deadline dates for each college.

If a family is depending on need-based financial aid to make their early decision, creating an accurate estimated CSS profile is critical. With the early decision acceptance letter, the student will receive a preliminary financial aid award letter. This financial award is the only way to decline the early acceptance. This early acceptance financial award is only an estimate and is not final until the FAFSA form is submitted and verified.

With this in mind, understanding your financial position is important. The results of your CSS submission will vary between colleges since each college has the opportunity to modify their calculation. Your FAFSA EFC number is the same at each college while it can vary greatly when using the CSS profile method.

In the rolling admission application process, the college will review applications as they are received. Schools that use the rolling admission method usually do not have cut-off dates for application. If students plans to use this process they should try to apply early as slots at each college may fill. This is especially true for certain academic majors within a college.

With rolling admissions, the complete financial award letter is normally available near April 1st. Some merit scholarships can be awarded during the rolling admission process.

The regular admission process is where students apply to a college by a certain deadline. Under this method, they will receive a decision no later than April 1 of their senior year of high school.

Excluding early decision, students will not have to make their final college decision until May 1st. These other methods allow families the ability to compare the net cost of each colleges of where they were accepted.

Starting October 2016, the colleges can receive both the application and FAFSA at the same time. This will change the admission and financial award letter process. At this time, it is unclear how each of the colleges will react and the information available to the student.

UNDERSTANDING YOUR FINANCIAL AID POSITION

Many parents of college-bound students feel anxious when completing the financial aid forms. Completing the FAFSA forms is required in order to get the expected family contribution number or EFC. The EFC number is generated after inputting your personal financial information into the FAFSA form. The process does require some detailed financial organization, but there is a lot of helpful information available to aid in this calculation. A good start would be to go to the government websites, https://fafsa.ed.gov/ or https://studentaid.ed.gov/.

Many people mistakenly believe that the EFC is one number. The actual calculation is really four separate numbers that are summed together: parents' income, parents' assets, student's income, and student's assets. Each of these components has separate rules and allowances.

A family will get their official EFC by completing the Free Application for Federal Student Aid or FAFSA. This process only provides you with one number and does not break out the four separate numbers. You need to understand the four quadrants of the EFC calculation to create a proper college-funding strategy.

> **Insider Note:**
>
> A popular myth is that you can reduce your EFC by taking all assets out of your child's name. This is not true. To make that decision, you need to understand the parent components of the EFC calculation and the cost of attendance of each college on the student's list. In some cases, it may be a better idea to put assets in the child's name to maximize tax savings.

The Department of Education provides your expected family contribution through two methods. The actual FAFSA process gives the family their EFC number after completing the form, while the FAFSA4caster is an estimate of your EFC number. Currently, neither of the government sources provides the four quadrant details of the EFC calculation.

Another place you can get your EFC calculation is on the EFCplus.com website. The website has a free simple EFC estimator and a more detailed EFC calculator is available as part of our EFC PLUS software.

The FAFSA process is also called the federal methodology. Any college or postsecondary education program that receives federal funds will require the student and family to submit a FAFSA form. This form has to be completed in order for the student to qualify for any federal financial aid. The exception to this rule is merit aid, which can be granted without any financial aid forms submitted.

Some colleges require a second financial aid process called the institutional methods. The most common of these methods is the CSS Profile managed by College Board. Generally, colleges that use a secondary process have a significant endowment that they are trying to distribute to their targeted applicants. The institutional methods will ask additional question beyond the FAFSA, and there is often a fee to use these methods.

The institutional methods are also used by schools that offer early decisions. The FAFSA process is available on October 1 of each year, so students who apply for early decision and need financial aid will need to use an institutional method. Each school is different. Parents and students should review the financial aid process and forms required. Being organized and meeting the deadlines helps the application process go more smoothly.

One of the biggest differences between the federal and institutional methodologies is how the colleges recognize the EFC numbers. The federal methodology value will be a fixed number at every school. The institutional method value will vary from college to college based on how each college develops their calculation. Most schools will not disclose your institutional number to you. This goes back to how schools use an admissions matrix to select their students and plan their revenue stream for the upcoming year. Remember, the matrix includes how much money you need and, indirectly, your ability to pay.

Methodology Differences

There is a great deal of confusion between the two methods. An important part of creating your funding strategy is determining your college list. If the colleges on your list do not include a CSS Profile school, you will not need to worry about completing the additional forms.

In general, the more competitive colleges use an institutional process. Over the past few years, the difference between the two methodologies has lessened. Listed in the table below are the major calculation differences between the federal and institutional methods.

Expected Family Contribution Method Comparison

Concept	FAFSA	CSS Profile/Institutional
General calculation	Same number for all colleges	Variable by college
Home equity	Not included	Most colleges include a percent
Retirement accounts	Not included	Can be included
Family business w less than 100 employees	Not included	Included
Non-custodial parent	Not included	Variable by college
Calculation allowances	Standard	Variable by college
Student contribution	Could be 0 value	Minimum expected

> **Insider Note:**
>
> **A list of schools that use the CSS Profile method can be found at https://profileonline.collegeboard.org.**

Classification of the Applicant

The majority of college-bound students will apply for financial aid as dependent students. This means students receive 50 percent of their living expenses through the support of a parent or guardian. These rules are very similar to the IRS rules when determining filing status of your taxes.

To qualify as an independent student, you must meet at least one of the following conditions:

- Be twenty-four years or older

- Be married

- At the beginning of the coming school year, be working on a master's or doctorate degree program (such as an MA, MBA, MD, JD, PhD, EdD, graduate certificate, etc.)

- Be currently serving on active duty in the US armed forces for purposes other than training (if you are a National Guard or reserves enlistee, you must be on active duty for other than state or training purposes)

- Be a veteran of the US armed forces

- Have—or will have—children who will receive more than half of their support from you prior to the application year you are applying for

- Have dependents (other than your children or spouse) who live with you and who receive more than half of their support from you, now and through the upcoming year

- At any time since you turned thirteen, both your parents were deceased, you were in foster care, or you were a dependent or ward of the court

- It has been decided by a court in your state of legal residence that you are an emancipated minor or that you are in a legal guardianship

- At any time on or after July 1 of the previous year, you were determined to be an unaccompanied youth who was homeless or self-supporting and at risk of being homeless, as determined by a) your high school or district homeless liaison, b) the director of an emergency shelter or transitional housing program funded by the US Department of Housing and Urban Development, or c) the director of a runaway or homeless youth basic center or transitional living program

Source: Department of Education

Insider Note:

The FAFSA and IRS systems are now linked. Inconsistencies between the two forms will raise a red flag during the information verification process. This is especially true for independent students and students of divorced/separated parents. Colleges will verify 30 to 100 percent of all financial aid applications.

The advantage of being an independent student is that the EFC will normally be lower. A lower EFC will provide increased financial aid for the student in most cases. An independent student will also get an increase in Stafford loan limits—this means an additional $4,000 of direct unsubsidized loans per year.

The independent student will not have the parents' quadrants to complete on the FAFSA form. As a result, the parents' assets and income will not be part of the EFC calculation. This could be an advantage.

In the past, some students tried to establish themselves as independent when they weren't. The rules are very strict now, and with the IRS link, it is almost impossible to achieve an independent classification without one of the requirements listed above.

Creating Your EFC Strategy

To create a college-funding strategy, you need to understand the details of the four EFC quadrants. A clear understanding of the quadrants helps families clarify the appropriate strategy to lower their out-of-pocket cost of education.

Once you have created your list of colleges, you will need the cost of attendance (or COA). This number will include tuition, fees, room and board, books, travel, and personal spending. The cost of attendance amount the school uses is an estimate and may not be what you actually need. As an example, if the student attends a school in California and lives in Pennsylvania, the travel cost home may be much higher than the amount included in a local college's COA.

You will then need your initial EFC number based on your current income and assets before any adjustments are made. Your most recent tax return is normally the best source for this information. Use the EFC calculator on www.EFCplus.com to calculate the quadrant values individually. The government websites are helpful but do not give you the four-quadrant breakout. Our calculator will also give you an estimate for both financial aid methods.

> **Insider Note:**
>
> **The key to qualifying for need-based financial aid is:**
>
> **COA – EFC = Financial Aid Need**

If your family's total EFC is greater than your COA, you will not qualify for need-based aid. However, you may still qualify for merit-based money depending on the strength of the student's application. If you have the details of the parents' part of the EFC calculation, you will be able to complete the full analysis.

If the parents' part of the EFC exceeds the college's COA, the value of the student's part of the EFC does not matter. When you know your numbers, you can see how it's not always advantageous to take all of the assets out of the student's name. This can be explained by the example below:

Parents' income EFC value:	$25,000
Parents' assets EFC value:	$12,000
Parents' EFC value	$37,000

Student's income EFC value:	$1,500
Student's assets EFC value:	$1,600
Student's EFC value	$3,100

Total EFC: **$40,100**

College One—COA: $31,000

No need-based aid

Moving student's assets will have no impact. Parent EFC of $37,000 is greater than College One COA of $31,000.

College Two—COA: $55,000
Qualify for $14,900 of need-based aid
Moving student's assets will have an impact. Parent EFC of $37,000 is less than College Two COA of $55,000.

With these examples, you can see how important it is to understand the details of the EFC numbers. Many middle-income families face the exact situation shown above. Most students' college lists will likely include schools for which they qualify for some need-based financial aid and other colleges where they will not.

Remember that the financial aspect is only one part of the college decision. The academics and campus culture are just as important in the decision process.

Insider Note:

Regardless of your financial situation, you should complete the FAFSA form. This will qualify the student for a Stafford loan, which is the sole legal responsibility of the student.

EFC Four Components

You have seen how the EFC works in the financial aid system. Now let's dive into the EFC components so you can better understand the major parts of each quadrant's calculation.

The first component is the parents' income; for most applicants this will be the largest number of the EFC. It is based on the family's structure, number of dependents, adjusted gross income, and state of residence. These terms are very similar to your federal tax terms, as the two systems are now linked together.

The parent income section of the calculation is progressive. As the family's Adjusted Gross Income increases, a higher percentage multiplier is put to that number. This will result in the EFC increasing more quickly.

> **Insider Note:**
>
> Under the FAFSA or federal method, in the years for which you apply for financial aid, any deferred compensation (e.g., 401K, 403b, and IRA contributions) gets added back in as income for financial aid purposes. For the income calculation of EFC, the value of the retirement account is not included. Only the employee's contribution is included. It still goes into the tax-deferred account. This is also true for the institutional method, but the retirement account value will be included in the asset section of that calculation. This information appears on the person's W2 or 1040 form.

For the parents' asset calculation, nonretirement assets are all included. Small farms, small family businesses and your home equity are also excluded. (*See methods table.*) There is an allowance amount based on the tax-filing status and the age of the oldest FAFSA-filing parent. The asset amount that exceeds the allocation amount will be multiplied by 5.67 percent to arrive at the parent asset calculated amount.

For dependent student income, the rules are very simple. Since dependent students are included on another person's tax return, their income allowances are limited by the state they reside in and the federal income exception amount. Amounts over the allowances are weighted at 50 percent.

For the student asset section, there are no allowances, and assets are weighted at 20 percent. This is why many people think it's a good idea to get assets out of the student's name. People compare the student percentage of 20 percent to the parents' percentage of 5.67 percent and disregard the cost of attendance as part of their decision. This is a common error.

Be careful when liquidating student assets. The first issue is the tax consequence of liquidating assets. For dependent college students up to the age of twenty-four, if there is a taxable gain from the sale of assets, the "kiddie tax" rules will apply. This means the first $2,100 (2016 limit) of unearned income will be tax-free, and any amount over that will be taxed at the parents' rate. This limit changes periodically based on the tax code. Depending on the amount of gain, a very high tax rate could be charged due to the parents' income level.

The next issue is ownership of the account or asset. If the primary social security number on the account is the student's, then it is legally their money. Legally this money must be spent on the student's behalf. You need to have documentation to properly liquidate a Uniform Gift to Minor Account (UGMA account), which is the type of account issued to most children under the age of eighteen.

Insider Note:

College saving plans, such as 529 plans, are reported as parent assets on the financial aid forms, not the students. All 529 money for all children must be reported on each FAFSA submission. This is often done incorrectly because the parent associated each account to each child. Because the parent has the right to change the beneficiary, all family 529 money must be reported. Grandparent or outside family 529 plans are not reported on the FAFSA but are required on the CSS Profile.

Timing Is Important

There are two important aspects of maximizing your financial aid award: The first is the timing of the financial decision for the FAFSA reporting, and the second is the impact of other siblings.

The FAFSA form becomes available on October 1 of each year and will be used for financial aid packages for students. The information used to complete the FAFSA form is based on the prior year's tax return.

The tax year and school year do not match. As an example, for entering college freshmen, the school years that will be used to complete the FAFSA are their second semester of sophomore year and their first semester of junior year of high school. With that understood, the best time to review your financial aid position is the tax year when your child is a second-semester sophomore and first-semester junior in high school.

It is also important to take into consideration when other siblings will be in college at the same time. The total EFC will be divided by the number of children in college. So if you have two in college, your EFC will be divided by two. Again, this is where a more expensive school may become affordable due to the change in EFC. This is another reason is why doing a four-year cash flow is important. This is how I help clients determine their best college value analysis.

Having a better understanding of your EFC will allow you to make a better financial decision. Doing a four-year cash analysis helps families project their total financial cost of college. Currently, most schools will only give you a one-year projection.

What is Prior Prior?

Starting October 1, 2016 a new method of submitting the FAFSA will start. Under the new Prior Prior FAFSA process, the EFC or Expected Family Contribution income numbers will be based on the tax year two years prior to submission. The new method will allow families to use the data retrieval tool (DRT) to download their income numbers from the IRS system in most cases. This will reduce the confusion on which tax information that needs to be included in the FAFSA submission. With this change, families will be able to get their EFC income number on October 1 of their senior year of high school. The student and parent will still need to input their assets but it will make the federal or FAFSA method easier.

As an example, the graduating high school class of 2017 will be using the 2015 taxes to complete the FAFSA. This is the reason why it is called Prior Prior. Due to this change, parents of younger students will need to move forward their financial positioning analysis. The best time to review a family's financial aid positioning will be before the student's 12/31 sophomore year in high school.

With the Prior Prior change, it does simplify some of the confusion regarding the income section of the FAFSA. Now families will be able to use the DRT system to populate sections of the FAFSA. The DRT system will work for most families excluding taxpayers who are still on extension or who have filed an amended tax return.

Creating a FSA ID

Before you start your FAFSA, the student and at least one parent must create their FSA ID. The FSA ID is the acronym for Federal Student Aid Identification. The FSA ID replaced the FAFSA Pin on May 10th, 2015. The FSA ID is the new login and electronic signature process that is replacing the current Federal Student Aid Pin used by the Department of Education. For students, parents and borrowers the FSA ID will be the electronic method used to apply for federal student aid and access any federal student aid records online. This new login process authenticates the user and allows them to access the following websites or processes:

- FAFSA on the Web

- NSLDS® Student Access

- StudentLoans.gov

- StudentAid.gov

- TEACH Grant

The new FSA ID login process will improve security since you create a user-selected username and password. The person will enter less information with this single sign-on process. The FSA ID will eliminate the need for people to enter personal identifiers such as Social Security, name and date of birth each time they want to login. This new change will give people a lifetime ID. The FSA ID is a similar process to most other secure login systems used for your banking and credit cards.

To establish the FSA ID go to:

https://fsaid.ed.gov/npas/index.htm

Insider Note

It is highly recommended that you create the FSA ID, yourself. The process requires two system security questions and two personal questions and answers. It also requires a date that is unique to you excluding your own birthday. Legally you should create your own FSA ID. It is your electronic signature.

Applying for Financial Aid

I have discussed the two method of applying for financial aid but have not described the process of applying. The applying process is determined by the student's college list. Once the college list and the method of applying is final, a list of financial aid deadlines should be created.

The CSS profile is available sometime in October for early decision applicants. If you are not applying under that method then refer to the regular deadlines for each college.

The FAFSA form is now available October 1 of each year. To complete and submit the FAFSA form the student and one parent will need a FSA ID. The FSA ID allows the student and parent to sign only the FAFSA form electronically.

I also recommend that everyone submit a FAFSA form no matter your financial strength. Just submitting this for the student will qualify them for a Direct Student Loan.

IRS Data Retrieval Tool

The IRS data retrieval tool (DRT) is available to parents who have completed a personal income tax submission with the IRS using the IRS form 1040, 1040A, or 1040EZ. This online DRT is able to transfer the tax-return information directly onto the FAFSA form. Using this tool is the easiest way to provide your tax information to the school. With the Prior Prior change you will be able to populate your income tax information directly into the FAFSA.

This tool updates the FAFSA information with the actual tax information that you have submitted to the IRS. It provides the actual income information to the school's financial aid office and prevents fraud. This new method eliminates the need to send copies of your tax returns to the college. Colleges that require the CSS Profile will still require you to submit various tax returns for multiple years. It is an important step in the verification process for the colleges in the financial aid process.

For some people, the DRT will not be available. This would include people with complicated tax returns, those who are still on extensions and anyone who had submitted an amended return for the tax year needed. If you are in that situation, you should contact the college to ask what information is required to complete the FAFSA verification. Many will require your tax transcript which is another IRS process that is more time consuming.

When and how you submit your taxes will impact when the information is available through the IRS system. It normally takes two to six weeks after the taxes are submitted before it is available to the DRT system. If you are on a payment plan or have a tax bill outstanding, your tax information will not be available for the DRT process.

To use the DRT tool, you need to enter through the online FAFSA form.
- Taxpayer must have filed a current tax return

  o Electronic submission method will provide better availability

- Taxpayer must have a valid Social Security number (SSN)

- Taxpayer must have signed up and created a federal student aid identification or FSA ID

- Taxpayer's address and name must exactly match those on the IRS Tax form

There are certain situations where the IRS DRT will not be available to be used for the FAFSA verification. They are as follows:

- Taxpayer is submitting an amended tax return

- Taxpayer is submitting for an extension

    o Once submitted, the verification will be done and the award will be reevaluated

- Taxpayer did not need to file a federal tax return

- Taxpayer filed a Puerto Rico or foreign income tax return

If the school wants verification of your taxes but you are unable to use the IRS DRT, you can get an official transcript form from the Internal Revenue Service. Go to www.irs.gov to find information and the form. It is always important to check with your school's financial aid department to make sure all your information has been received according to the deadlines listed.

Insider Note:

All FAFSA forms and federal student loans will require an electronic signature by the student and parent. The student and parent will need to obtain a FSA ID.

Student Aid Report (SAR)

The Student Aid Report is the confirmation report that is generated after the FAFSA is submitted. It is the information that will be sent to the colleges. Normally it is available 2 – 5 days after the FAFSA is submitted. It is highly recommended that you review this report to confirm your submitted information.

This is also a big difference between the FAFSA and Institutional financial aid methods. The SAR confirms your information and generates the Expected Family Contribution or EFC. The Federal EFC is the same number at every college. The Institutional EFC will vary by college and is often not disclosed to the student and family.

DEVELOPING A COLLEGE SAVING PLAN

Paying for their children's college education is a top goal for most parents, but this is becoming more difficult to achieve. According to a 2013 Department of Agriculture report, the average cost to raise a child from birth to eighteen years is $241,080.[4] Depending on where you live in the United States, this number could actually be higher.

At the same time, the median household income has fallen nearly $4,000 after adjusting for inflation since 2000. This financial stress can make saving for college very difficult for many families. According to the Labor Department (data compared prices from August of 2003 to 2013), the college tuition price index has increased over twice that of medical costs. If you compare it to the overall consumer price index, the increase is significantly worse.[5]

A family's ability to pay is becoming a factor in some admission decisions at various colleges. Many families tend to overlook this fact. They hope that scholarships and financial aid will make college affordable but this is often not the case. Student debt is now well over $1.2 trillion and growing. The debt burden will affect our children's ability to buy homes and start families in the future. Better financial decisions need to be made during this process.[6]

I often get questions about saving for college at my speaking engagements, including from parents who have saved nothing for college. They want to know if they will qualify for more financial aid because of their financial status. While having no savings may show that you have more need, there is no guarantee that the school will provide all of the money you need to attend that college.

Let's revisit the parents' quadrant of the EFC calculation: The parent has an allowance based on the age of the oldest parent filing the FAFSA and his or her tax-filing status. The parents' savings has the smallest impact on the expected family contribution number.

As an example, a person who has saved nothing would have zero assets and a zero parent asset value in the EFC calculation. But now take a parent who is married, files a joint tax return, and is fifty years old. According to the 2014 FAFSA parent asset allowance table, that family could have $34,600 in assets and still have a zero EFC from the assets saved. It is important to understand that the first family will need to borrow more funds at the parent's interest rate. The Parent PLUS (a type of loan that will be discussed in detail below) rate is much higher and has higher fees than the student rate. Again, knowing your numbers can help you avoid costly mistakes before and during your planning process.

The Cost of Not Saving

I explained how having some savings can still result in a low or zero EFC portion on the parent asset calculation, but let's really look at the full consequences of not saving.

Let us take a family who can save $200 per month for ten years in a 529 saving plan with an annual return of 7 percent. This will eliminate the consequence of taxes because the growth would be tax-free and have no impact when you liquidate the funds. The projected total of this investment would be $34,819.

Now we have the family who was not able to save or decided not to save. They will need to borrow that money. That same $34,819 at an interest rate of 6.8 percent would have a monthly payment of $401. That is double the monthly saving amount. This example shows you the impact of compounding interest. It also displays how both families would have the same parent asset number in the EFC calculation.

> **Insider Note:**
>
> The amount students can borrow under the federal loan system is limited by year and is not that high. Based on current college costs, the majority of student borrowers will require a loan for which the parent is a cosigner and legally responsible. This includes the Parent PLUS loan and other personal loans.

Where to Begin

As a parent, you need to look at a few things before you start saving for college. Priorities may be different for each family, but all of these items need to be considered before you create your plan:

- Number of years before first child goes to college

- Age of the parents when the last child graduates from college

- Amount that can be saved per month

- Retirement funding

- Educational-funding gifts

- Estimated goal by child

This process can be daunting, but the sooner you start analyzing your unique financial situation, the sooner you can develop a strategy for paying for college. I see this lack of planning illustrated through the growing college debt levels. To help your children reach a level of independence, you need to make this a priority as a parent.

Before you rush out and try to find the right investment option, first establish a timeline. This will identify a few things for you:

- Recovery time for retirement saving

- Beneficial financial aid position based on multiple children in college (lower EFC)

- Amount of time when tuition is payable

- Priority levels of retirement and college saving goals

By understanding the timing, you can then determine which investment options will be the most beneficial. You may need to have a combination of retirement tools and college saving tools to attain both goals.

Saving Options

Due to the unique resources, priorities, and goals of each family, it would be impossible to provide an answer for every possible situation. However, this section will list the most common college savings options. As described, these savings options are for *college-funding* use only. Some of these investments have other personal financial benefits that will not be described but will need to be considered in your decision process. Each investment needs to be evaluated based on how it will affect your educational goals and other personal financial purposes.

When weighing investment options, consider the cost of each investment, the ability to access the funds, and any associated penalties. This is a very complicated personal financial decision; make sure your viewpoint is broad before you make the investment. Focusing on only one aspect, such as lowering your EFC, may cost you more in the long run because you may not be able to access the funds (without incurring a large penalty), and you may also need to borrow money to pay tuition.

Student Saving Account (UGMA or UTMA)

This is an account that is in the student's name with a person assigned as a custodian of the account. The account funds must be spent for the benefit of the child. It is under this legal structure to protect the child. Depending on the state, the account becomes the child's money at age eighteen or twenty-one. This can be a bank savings account, checking account, or investment account.

Pro: This account will have a tax advantage, especially for high-income families. If the parents' EFC is higher than the college COA, it will have no impact on their financial aid position.

   If properly used, this account can deliver a zero income tax opportunity for appreciated assets. This requires some advanced tax and liquidating strategies.

Con: Assets in the student's name are weighted at 20 percent in the financial aid or EFC calculation.

   Understanding the components of the EFC and college cost need to be calculated before liquidation occurs. If you liquidate the funds, you need to be aware of the "kiddie tax" rules, and the funds must be used for the child's benefit.

Insider Note:

The "kiddie tax" rules affect dependent college students under the age of twenty-four. A certain amount of unearned income is tax-free depending on the IRS limit (2016 current limit $2,100).. Any amount above that limit will be taxed at the parent's income tax rate depending on the investment.

US Saving Bonds

This is an investment that has the full backing of the US federal government and grows with interest that is earned based on the type of bond and the month it was purchased. This investment is often given as a gift to younger children with the expectation of tax-free growth for education.

Pro: For education purposes, some or all of the accumulated interest may be tax-free.

Con: Tax-free education rules are often poorly understood. To receive tax-free growth, the US saving bond must be in the name of the parent and have a certain income limit based on how the parent files his or her taxes. These income limits change periodically based on IRS rules.

529 Plans

This type of plan is operated by the state and designed to help families save for future college costs. As long as the plan satisfies the requirements, the federal tax law will provide special tax benefits to the plan participant and beneficiary of the plan (section 529 of the Internal Revenue Code).

It is up to each state to decide whether it will offer a 529 plan (or possibly more than one) and what it will look like. The 529 plans are usually categorized as either prepaid or savings, although some have elements of both.

Pro: Grows tax-free if used for qualified education expenses. Some states offer an income tax deduction for contributions to their plans. Different investment options exist within these plans, both on a risk-level and age-based portfolio basis.

These plans can be passed down among family members. All 529 plans are reported as parent assets for financial aid calculations when held by the parents and student of the family.

Con: You can only make one investment change in the portfolio per year within the same plan administrator.

     This investment can only be used for qualified educational expenses to get the tax-free growth. It cannot be used for student-loan repayment.

Insider Note:

Many believe that a 529 plan is only a precollege investment option. If your state's 529 plan offers an income tax deduction benefit, it can also be considered an investment option during college. Make sure you understand your state's 529 benefits before you invest in another state's plan.

Coverdell Saving Plan

This investment option, also called an Educational IRA, can be used for college and also for tuition expenses of elementary and secondary school. There is a contributor income limit and investment amount limit per child per year from all sources.

Pro: These plans offer more investment flexibility than the 529 plans.

     These are considered a parents' asset in the financial aid calculation.

     It can be converted into a 529 plan to receive an in-state tax deduction (if offered) and continue growing tax-free.

Con: The plan needs to be used by the student before age thirty for qualified educational expenses.

     The maximum contribution from all sources is $2,000 per year from all sources.

Parent Investment Portfolio

This is a general investment tool. The investment goes into the account with after-tax money and offers investment flexibility.

Pro: This option allows parents to save for any financial goal.

There are some tax advantages to transferring the portfolio to the student if he or she does not qualify for need-based financial aid.

It can be used for college fees, loan repayment, and any other personal financial goals.

Con: It is counted in the federal EFC calculation and CSS Profile method as a parent asset.

Roth IRA

This is primarily a retirement saving investment option. The investment goes into the account with after-tax money. After five years, these contributions are available for educational expenses if correctly withdrawn. There are specific contribution rules set by the IRS that may limit your ability to use this option.

Pro: This option allows parents to save for both retirement and college.

It is not counted in the federal EFC calculation, but it is reported under the CSS method.

It has great investment flexibility and grows tax-free.

This is a good option to consider when you have younger children.

Con: Income and participation rules may not allow you to use this option.

Money must be in the plan for five years before you can access it.

Traditional IRA Account

This is a retirement saving investment option. The investment goes into the account with tax-deferred money. There are specific contribution rules set by the IRS that may limit your ability to use this option.

Pro: Account value is not counted in the federal EFC calculation, but it is reported under the CSS method.
It has great investment flexibility and grows tax deferred. The 10 percent early withdrawal penalty is waived if used for qualified educational expenses.

Con: Participation rules may not allow you to use this option.
A withdrawal for qualified educational expenses may come out without the pre-withdrawal penalty, but income tax will be charged on it. These withdrawals will be reported as income on your tax return and increase your EFC the following year.
Contributions to these plans in the years you are applying for financial aid are reported as income in the EFC calculation.

Company Retirement Account

This is a retirement saving investment option. The investment goes into the account with tax-deferred money. There are specific contribution rules set by the IRS that may limit your ability to use this option.

Pro: Account value is not counted in the federal EFC calculation, but it is reported under the CSS method.
It has good investment flexibility and grows tax deferred.
Loan options are available and are normally limited to $50,000 or less based on account value.

Con: Withdrawals from these accounts are loans and not reported as income on your tax return. When you have a loan against your company retirement plan and are laid off or leave the company, the outstanding balance needs to be paid back within sixty days. If the outstanding balance is not paid back, the amount will be reported as income and will increase your EFC the following year.

Contributions to these plans, in the years you are applying for financial aid, are reported as income in the EFC calculation.

Cash Value Life Insurance

This is a personal financial risk investment option. Contributions to these investments are normally expensive and are used as a tax-deferred method of growth. This type of insurance is sometimes promoted as a college-funding option. It is important to understand your financial position and the overall advantages of this option.

Pro: Account value is not counted in the federal EFC calculation, but it is reported under the CSS method.

Con: Once the money is invested, there is limited access and a cost to get access to your funds. To receive the full benefits of the investment, this needs to be a long-term decision, not a short-term solution. Based on your EFC asset value, your ability to pay tuition, and the cost of making the investment, this investment option is often less attractive for short-term strategies.

Annuities

This is a personal financial risk and retirement investment option. Contributions to these investments are normally expensive and are used as a tax-deferred method of growth. This investment is sometimes promoted as a college-funding option, but you need to understand your numbers and determine the advantages of this option.

Pro: Account value is not counted in the federal EFC calculation, but it is reported under the CSS method.

Con: Once the money is invested, there is limited access and a cost to get access to your funds. To receive the full benefits of the investment, it needs to be part of a long-term decision and not a short-term solution. Based on your EFC asset value, your ability to pay tuition, and the cost of making the investment, in many cases this investment becomes less attractive.

Insider Note:

The financial aid process requires the family to open their entire financial life. Some financial advisors use this opportunity to promote life insurance and annuity as college-funding solutions. You need to know your EFC, especially the parents' EFC asset number and the final impact of that investment. In many cases the cost of borrowing the money will make that solution unattractive. If you plan to use insurance and annuities as a college-funding vehicle, understand the withdrawal cost and penalties before making the investment.

Trust Beneficiary

This is a general investment tool normally set up by another family member. The investment goes into the account with after-tax money and offers investment flexibility. Many trusts are setup for complex personal reasons and will normally have other personal financial goals.

Pro: This option allows the trustee to control the distribution of assets over a specified time period.

Con: It is counted in the federal EFC calculation and CSS Profile method. The asset value is reported by the listed beneficiary. Often set up as a simple solution for estate planning, this type of investment disregards the financial aid position of the individual family members.

Outside Resources and Other Family Members

It is really a great advantage if you are lucky enough to have family members or friends willing to help with your children's educational funding. There is a great deal of confusion in this area, especially for grandparents. Many grandparents need to balance their retirement funding and estate planning with this educational goal. Grandparents who want to gift money to multiple grandchildren should do some advance planning. The gifting solution may be different for each family that they want to help. Each family may have a different EFC number, resulting in a different college strategy for each grandchild and family.

A common area of confusion is how educational investment accounts are titled. With the IRS system and FAFSA system now linked, financial and tax information will be more transparent. As an example, if a grandparent is the owner of a 529 saving plan, and it is used for qualified expenses, it may show up under the student's IRS information as untaxed income. If this student qualifies for need-based financial aid, this transaction could increase his or her EFC and reduce aid in the following year. At this point, colleges have not pursued this ability, but they have the capability now.

> **Insider Note:**
>
> **The 529 plan of the grandparent does not need to be reported under the FAFSA method, but it is reported under the CSS Profile method.**

What happens if an outside resource pays for tuition directly to the college? If the student qualifies for need-based aid, this could reduce the aid dollar for dollar. This occurs most frequently when a grandparent or friend tries to reduce assets for estate-planning purposes. Tuition is one of the few items that can exceed the gift tax limits if it is paid to the college directly.

More advanced strategies of gifting can be considered depending on the state residency of both the gift giver and the gift receiver. The receiver could be the parents, the child, or both, depending on the amount of money.

To help families maximize their financial resources, some advanced personal financial planning should be considered. Certain decisions can affect a family's financial aid position significantly.

Insider Note:

Senior citizens who want to help with college costs need to be careful about how the money is gifted. If at some point they need Medicaid assistance, the past five years of their financial history will be examined. If this history includes large financial gifts, this may affect their eligibility to receive Medicaid benefits immediately.

Planning Summary

As you can see, there are various options to consider. When creating a college saving plan, you need to evaluate other items, such as retirement and financial aid timing. Having a priority list of your goals will improve your decision process.

Insider Note:

Before engaging a college financial planner, here are a few things to consider:

- The advisor should be a fiduciary. This means the advisor must act in your best interest.

- Understand how the advisor is compensated, whether based on fees or on recommended solutions. (I prefer a fee-only advisor as the best option.)

- Check whether a third party will process the analysis for the advisor. You need to disclose your entire financial life in this process. Another person or company accessing your confidential information may increase the risk of identity theft.

- Use this book to ask a few technical questions. See if the financial planner can answer them and if he or she is an expert in the area of college funding. Many financial planners have a general knowledge of college funding but not specific expertise with the various strategies.

CREATING A PAYING FOR COLLEGE STRATEGY

Paying for college is not just a matter of financial aid. Many parents believe the only way to lower their college cost is through the financial aid process. This is not true. Every year I hear a new trick for getting more financial aid, and most are not valid. In addition to the financial aid process, there are college saving plans, educational tax credits, and financing options that in combination can save you thousands of dollars each year. Various educational funding strategies can be developed depending on your income level, EFC number, and the colleges being considered.

I have explained how financial aid positioning works and how to save for college, but the college selection decision can be the most important in the process. To select the best college, there are three things to consider: the perfect college fit needs to meet academic goals, provide an engaging environment, and be affordable for the family. These items will need to be weighted equally in the decision process.

The academic and environmental aspects are somewhat subjective decisions, while the financials have a more defined process. Be careful not to minimize the financial aspects with the expectation of easy access to student loans. Student loans are some of the easiest loans to get approval for, but they are also one of the most difficult to eliminate. Most students do not realize how quickly the loans can accumulate while they are being incurred.

My perspective on the college decision is somewhat different and maybe old-fashioned. I try to get my clients to focus on the outcome of the education, not just on admission. Today, many careers require an education beyond the undergraduate degree. This is an added expense that needs to be considered as soon as possible in the college decision process.

Pursuing a college education has been described as a life experience, or at least it is marketed that way by some colleges. This can be a very expensive life experience, especially when you consider that education costs continue to outpace inflation, and student debt is rising at an alarming rate. Parents and students should be aware that graduation rates are declining, as is the quality of employment opportunities. At times, I think we have lost sight of the practical reasons for a college education.

From the viewpoint of a college financial planner, this is one of the most complicated financial decisions facing parents. I feel there is not enough financial literacy assistance provided for students and parents to fully understand the financial consequences of their college decisions.

Pre-decision Preparation Mistakes

Many students will take a challenging course load, get good grades, take standardized test preparation courses, and do extra curriculum activities so that their application will look attractive. All of these items are very important from an admission standpoint, but further steps in the college affordability process are often overlooked.

For comparison reasons, let us use the student loan approval process and compare it to the first time homebuyer.

Consider first-time homebuyers who want everything. They have saved money for the down payment, they have maintained a good credit score, they have a steady paying job, and they want to purchase a home in a certain area with specific amenities. Yet when they apply for a mortgage, it will be reviewed by the bank, and outsiders will determine through a variety of financial ratios if they are willing to take the risk of loaning money to these prospective homebuyers. The question is will these buyers be able to afford this mortgage or loan payment in the future.

For federal student loans, this process is almost nonexistent. There are some loan limits depending on the loan type, but there is no review process or affordability ratio. The review process in most other personal borrowing is rigorous. The reason for this easy access is that it is very difficult to eliminate this loan debt through bankruptcy. Parent PLUS loans and private loans have a review process, but it is not nearly as thorough as other personal loans.

There is a different mind-set when it comes to borrowing money for educating your children. Many students and families under estimate the affect of the student debt after graduation. I believe the approach and mind-set needs to change.

We can see how inefficient this industry is on a national level with a graduation rate of approximately 40 percent after four years. On an individual school level, the graduation rates and outcomes can be very different. The issue is that consumers have an extremely high level of trust in the college industry. However, in recent years more families have begun to question the real cost and value of a college education. The goal of this book is exactly that.

Listed below are some strategies you can use to minimize risk and maximize your resources for paying for college. Each child and family situation is different; depending on your situation, you may need to combine several strategies to create your plan.

- Improve your financial literacy

- Understand the difference between merit and need-based financial aid

- Calculate your financial aid position

- Create a four-year funding analysis

- Analyze all of the financing options

- Comparing value on an outcome basis not just sticker price

- Understanding the award letter

- Use all of the educational tax strategies properly

- Project loan repayment and forgiveness amounts

Improve Your Financial Literacy

As tuitions have risen and the level of financial aid complexity has increased, the financial literacy of students, parents, and financial professionals has not kept up. Many of the decisions young adults are making will affect their future personal and financial lives for many years. Most high school and college students are not provided with a financial education or seek the proper advice that is needed. In many cases, their knowledge on the topic is self-taught. This is concerning based on the amount of money it can cost to attend college and get a degree.

Insider Note:

Due to the increase cost more colleges are adding financial literacy programs. This may be a program or service you look for during your college visits. The EFC PLUS blog, video library, webinars and calculator can be valuable tools in the financial decision process.

Many students understand that they need a college education to achieve their dream job, but many do not worry about paying for this education until after graduation. No one explains to students the financial outcome of obtaining that education. Colleges only provide financial information one year at a time, which makes comparing actual value difficult for most students and families.

A major reason why I wrote this book is the lack of financial planning done by students and families. I hear from many of our loan repayment clients who wish they could turn back the clock and make better financial decisions. Many are living with college financial repayments that they did not realize at the time of their decision. They did not envision the financial outcome of their education.

Insider Note:

Students and parents need to change their approach to the college financial decision. They need to look at the college investment on a four-year basis and not as a one-year decision. Our EFC PLUS software does this. It helps you project the financial outcome and debt level after the degree is earned. It shows how your resources are used by year and then projects the additional amount of money you will need to get to graduation and the repayment amounts.

Financially, it's a good idea to select a major as soon as possible. Investigate the options with a visit to the college career center—an important part of the college visit and decision. Being proactive in selecting a career early will minimize the risk of additional semesters and their associated cost. Information needs to be gathered by career, taking into account the income level of the future job compared to the quality of life the student is trying to achieve. A reality check of the supply and demand for each career will also need to be evaluated.

At my speaking engagements, I suggest envisioning the student's life at twenty-five. By that age, the student has completed the majority of their education and has begun working. They are in the real world as an adult with personal and financial responsibilities.

This can be difficult, especially for an eighteen-year-old to comprehend. Parents need to monitor their children's decisions as they go through the college process so that they have a positive college experience and outcome. If you just look at the graduation rates, it seems a great deal of effort is required to keep students on track.

As an example, with all three of my daughters, we discussed the career opportunities and financial rewards of the degrees they were pursuing, the positives and negatives of each career considered, what their future employers might expect educationally and academically from them, and whether they could improve their resumes in any way before graduation. A college degree is sometimes not enough; employers expect more today.

Delaying talking to your child may result in added costs and possible lost income. As parents, I feel you need to focus on the outcome. You need to provide the information the child will need to make better decisions in adulthood. In most cases, this is your money and your investment in their future and their independence.

Understand the Different Types of Financial Aid

It is extremely important to review the student's list of colleges to determine the net costs associated with each school. Most colleges have two types of financial aid: merit based and need based financial aid. Sometimes it is hard to distinguish between the two when you get your financial award letter. If you're uncertain, it's best to contact the college and make sure you understand the award letter.

Merit-based financial aid is free money that is not determined by your financial aid position or EFC. This is considered a scholarship and can be awarded to a student for a variety of reasons, usually for academics or special skills that the student will bring to that college. Students normally receive a separate letter explaining the scholarship and the amount they will receive over the four years. For need-based students a merit scholarship can be part of the entire financial award package.

As an example, the scholarship letter will state something like: "Congratulations. You have received the Presidential Scholarship worth $40,000. It will result in a $10,000 reduction of tuition per year."

This rewards students for their hard work and serves as an incentive from the college to attract the best students. As I described earlier, each school tries to create a certain class profile; colleges use merit awards to attract the students they want.

If your child receives a merit-award letter, you need to do some additional work. Some awards will describe the minimum requirements of the merit scholarship, for example, maintaining a certain GPA level. The student needs to understand the rules and consequence of each award. Depending on the college, if that GPA level is not maintained, the entire scholarship may be at risk, or it may be prorated. Either way, it will cost the student more money to attend that college in that year and possibly the next.

In most cases, merit scholarship money is only applied to full-time students. If this is the case, learn what full time means at the college your child attends. Falling below full-time status could affect the scholarship. For example, students who decide to take an internship during the school year may need to enroll in evening or online courses to keep the credit criteria for their scholarship. Problems can also arise if a student decides to drop a couple of classes without picking up new ones. It is important to know the rules of the merit scholarships.

Insider Note:

From a financial standpoint, no matter what the financial situation, students should have two or three colleges on their list in which they are in the top 20 percent of the application pool from an academic level. This will improve the student's ability to receive merit-based financial aid at those specific colleges.

When creating your list of schools, ensure you have a good sense of where your child is in the academic field. The Academic and Financial Aid Matrix explained in chapter 2 visualize where a student is on a particular school's academic scale. Academics are one of the most important parts of the matrix, but schools are looking for a variety of other things to complete that class profile. Criteria such as the college essay, the state in which the student resides, or being the first generation of the family to attend college can improve a student's admissions attractiveness. Each school weighs the various parts of the application differently.

The merit-based process is extremely important for high-income and high-net-worth families. Merit-based aid may be the only way for these families to reduce tuition costs from the college. There are other ways to save money, but that money will not come from the college. There are strategies for high-net-worth families to save money, but they require a professional that has expertise in the financial aid process, taxes, and educational investments.

Need-based aid is a little different because it takes into account your financial situation. From an admission standpoint, the college is still focusing on creating the ideal class profile. At the same time, that class profile needs to generate a level of income to pay the bills of the college. Most colleges face this dilemma when creating the best mix of accepted students.

I describe earlier how the expected family contribution was calculated. The EFC is an important part of the need-based financial aid calculation. The first part of the need calculation is determining if you have financial need at a college. If your EFC number is less than the COA number, you qualify for need-based financial aid.

Insider Note:

Here is an example: College COA - EFC = Need

$30,000 - $20,000= $10,000

This calculation for need-based aid is the same for every school under the federal or FAFSA method. Since the college's COA number will be different for each school, the need-based aid at each college will change.

When comparing a state school with a private school, a family's financial need could be very different. This is where additional analysis is required since the private college may be able to provide additional financial aid making the net prices more comparable.

Remember, when you are comparing value; you also need to consider graduation rates and retention in the financial aspects of the college decision.

Insider Note:

Under the federal method or FAFSA, your EFC will be the same at every school. If some of the schools require the institutional method, each college adjusts its EFC calculation. Your FAFSA EFC is the same, but the institutional EFC will be different. In most cases, the institutional EFC will not be disclosed to you. The college will normally use the higher of the two EFC numbers.

Here is a series of examples to help you better understand how the amount of need you have changes based on the student's list of colleges:

Table 1

College	F/A Method	COA -	EFC =	Need	Qualify For Need Based Aid
College 1	FAFSA Only	19,000	20,000	NA	No
College 2	FAFSA Only	30,000	20,000	10,000	Yes
College 3	FAFSA/ CSS				
	FAFSA	50,000	20,000	30,000	Yes
	CSS	50,000	28,000	22,000	Yes

Notice the FAFSA EFC did not change at any of the colleges, and the CSS Profile number was different from the FAFSA number at College Three.

The next part of the need analysis is somewhat subjective and is not normally disclosed by the colleges. I have mentioned some of the factors why certain student may get more aid depending on the students' application and the schools goals for a given year. When I analyze this for clients, I use the historical averages for that college to determine a family's projected financial aid. This method reduces some of the uncertainty within the process and gives the client a starting point.

Each college will only meet a certain part of a family's need, and only a certain percentage of that will be gift aid, or free money.

In the table above, College Two lists family need at $10,000. We will say that the average need amount met by this college is 75 percent, and 80 percent of this amount will be gift aid. Here is how this would look:

College Two will give the family a $7,500 package ($10,000 x 75 percent) of which $6,000 (80 percent) will be free money, and the balance of $1,500 will be in the form of repayable loans and work-study. In this example the net cost to attend this college would be $24,000 ($30,000–$6,000).

Below is a brief example of how different colleges meet different percentages, provided in order to help you understand the financial value of each college. The table cannot provide an overall value because you need to consider the academics and environment of each school before you make your decision.

Table 2

College	F/A Method	Need	% Need Met	% Gift Aid	% Self Help	Estimate Free Money
College 1	FAFSA	0	50%	40%	60%	No
College 2	FAFSA	10,000	75%	80%	20%	$6,000
College 3	FAFSA/ CSS					
	FAFSA	30,000				
	CSS	22,000	90%	80%	20%	$15,840

In table 2, I have brought down only the amount needed at each college. College Three is a little different because it requires the CSS Profile. As mentioned, the CSS Profile would normally use the higher of the two

EFC numbers when determining need and award. In table 1, College Three has an EFC of $20,000 for the FAFSA and $28,000 under the CSS Profile. Since the CSS Profile EFC number is higher, the family only qualifies for $22,000 of need and not $30,000.

Colleges that use a secondary financial aid process protect their methodology very closely. Colleges that use the institutional method adjust their calculation each year. These adjustments are made so that they can attract the best students for their school.

You may think it is unfair for the colleges to take this secretive approach. Remember this is business. Would Coke tell Pepsi about its new marketing plan? Of course not, and the colleges are no different. They compete for the best students they can get to complete their desired class profile and generate the income they need to stay open. Most students or families do not understand this part of the acceptance process.

The college admission and financial aid packaging decisions can change from year to year, creating confusion for the consumer and a lot of misinformation. From a different perspective, the way colleges select students is the same as a company selecting employees or a team picking players.

> **Insider Note:**
>
> Colleges use their financial aid packaging to assist in their admission process. This is called "preferential packaging." The allocation of college money is given to the students whom the school is trying to attract. This is done in order to achieve class-demographics and a certain revenue goals.

Knowing the projected financial aid for each school will help you to narrow the list of colleges to the ones the family can afford. However, while knowing the average financial aid package can give you some insights into what a school can provide, remember that the actual award can vary greatly by student for a variety of reasons.

Developing Your Cost of Attendance (COA)

Understanding the cost of attending the college of your choice is an important aspect of your college strategy. This begins with gathering all of the fees to attend the college. Some of these costs are billed directly from the school to the parent, and others are incurred directly by the student. There are also expenses that parents have to incur that are not included in the COA.

From a need-based financial aid perspective, it is important to know the cost of attendance that the college is using to determine a family's financial need. Most schools have a standard number that is used depending on the student's residency. You need to create your own personal budget and compare it to what the school uses. Your expenses could be higher than the school's COA and result in a higher out-of-pocket cost to you.

The direct expenses are fairly easy to determine. They are typically tuition, fees, room, and board. Room-and-board expenses will vary depending on the housing options you have selected. For many large state universities, on-campus living is limited to only the first few years with off-campus living expected during the remaining education timeframe. Future off-campus living is still viewed as part of the cost of attendance for that college.

Indirect expenses, such as books, personal living expenses, and travel will vary greatly between schools. This is an important part to work on when trying to project your financial budget.

An indirect bill that is not included in the cost of attendance is the parents' expenses to visit or participate in activities at the college during the school year. This also needs to be considered as an expense when creating your college budget.

Insider Note:

If you are considering colleges that are far from home, it's a good idea to create a detailed budget that includes travel, time, and methods of transportation.

Create a Four-Year Financial Plan

In my opinion, the biggest weakness in the college-funding decision process is the way financial information is provided to families. Colleges and most families only look at the financial commitment on a one-year basis. This is a significant error. For many parents, this is one of the largest investments in their children they will ever make; better financial planning is needed.

Insufficient funding is one of the most common reasons for students' leaving college. A lot of emotions are associated with the initial college decision. Many times the long-term funding view is minimized and not properly thought out. Having a four year plan can reduce the risk of added cost.

It can be shortsighted, and potentially much more expensive than you think. Students who need to transfer colleges may lose credits or need to retake classes already paid for. The consequences can be even greater for students who do not complete their degrees: debt may have been incurred without a degree to show for it.

In both cases, the impact of not analyzing the financial commitment correctly can compound quickly.

> **Insider Note:**
>
> Approximately 30 percent of students transfer within the first year. Because some college credits are not transferable, this will cause a delay in graduation and add more cost. If you factor in the delay in getting a paying job, this becomes an additional opportunity cost (National Student Clearinghouse Research Center, July 10, 2014).

Creating a four-year cash flow by college is also important since it allows you to compare the true projected net cost of each college. This is especially true if you have multiple children in college at the same time, which could reduce your EFC significantly. It may allow you to qualify for more need-based financial aid, resulting in a lower net price.

When you see the financial outcomes listed by college, you can more easily compare the other important aspects of the college decision, including the academic strengths and the environment of the colleges considered.

As an example, many private colleges meet a higher percentage of financial need, and a greater amount of that is gift aid. This can make a private college much more affordable than a lower-sticker-priced state university.

Of course the financial side isn't the only consideration. Some clients see that a state university is less expensive, but they feel that their child will not be able to learn in a larger academic environment. Throughout this book I have mentioned that parents and students need to focus on the outcome of the education. This may include the learning environment and the cost of attaining a specific degree. When you factor in the graduation rates, retention, and possible additional financial aid, a private institution can offer a better value. You need to calculate the numbers to compare the real value and total cost of each college.

Another advantage of the four-year cash flow is that it enables you to see what debt will be incurred. Depending on a family's financial resources and goals, how the money is borrowed will vary greatly.

Most families do not realize that students can borrow a limited amount under their name only. If they need more money to pay for tuition, a parent will need to take out PLUS loans or private loans. Most loans, other than federal direct student loans, will require the signature of the parent or another cosigner. Parents can also take out PLUS loans for their child, but these are the legal responsibility of the parent.

An important outcome of creating a four-year cash flow is identifying the years when additional resources will be required to attend that college. In most cases, a student and family will need to borrow to cover the shortfall. With this information, you can make better borrowing decisions, taking into consideration the various loan options and their advantages and disadvantages.

With this cash-flow concept in mind, taking the Student Direct loans (formally called Stafford) early in the college-funding process may be recommended. This concept goes against the conventional thought process since most times you want to delay borrowing the money for as long as possible. However, if the student borrows the money at the very beginning, parents will minimize the amount of debt in their names at graduation. In addition, the student-loan interest rate is lower and the loan repayment options are better for the student than for the parents.

By understanding how the debt will be structured, you can project what your monthly payment will be at graduation. If you are able to do this during your decision process, the four-year methodology will improve your decision making process.

KNOWING YOUR PAYING OPTIONS

Once you have received your acceptance letter and depending on the method you used to apply, the colleges will provide to you a financial aid award letter. In most cases you will receive this information by April 1st for entering freshman.

The award letter will consist of merit and need-based aid as well as grants and loans. Grants are "free money" usually based on need and provided by the federal or state government and colleges. Federal, state, and college grants are based on the student's FAFSA EFC number and the cost of attendance of each college. Awards can vary greatly by school for a variety of reasons. In addition, the format of the award letter is not consistent across colleges.

Listed below are the most common lines items that appear on a student's financial aid award letter. If you are unclear on a specific item, it is recommended that you contact the financial aid office at that specific college.

The Federal Pell Grant

The Pell grant is funded through the federal government and awarded to a student based on the family's income and the EFC calculation. The Department of Education allocates this money to low-income families, and the money does not need to be paid back. For a student to be eligible, the family's yearly income must be lower than $50,000.

The maximum award for a Pell grant in the award year July 1, 2016 to June 30, 2017 is $5,815 per year.

Federal Supplemental Educational Opportunity Grant (FSEOG)

The FSEOG is a federal grant awarded to undergraduate students based on financial need and academic progress. This is sometimes called *campus-based aid* and is administered directly by the college and the federal government. Not every school participates, so please check with your college's financial aid office to see if your college offers the FSEOG.

Students can receive grants for between $100 and $4,000 per year. The college manages it with specific rules determined by the federal government.

State Grants

Students may receive state grants if they meet the eligibility requirements for the state and if they are determined to have need based on their FAFSA. Reciprocal states may have agreements with each other. The grant is administered by the state, and the amount is based on how much funding the state has in its budget. The amount can vary and is determined by both the need amount and the tuition amount. To maximize this benefit, attending an in-state college can be more beneficial.

> **Insider Note:**
>
> The following website lists the state grant agencies:
>
> http://www2.ed.gov/about/contacts/state/index.html

Teacher Education Assistance for College and Higher Education (TEACH) Grant Program

TEACH is a federal grant of up to $4,000 a year that can be obtained by students planning to teach children from low-income families or in high-need fields. One of the criteria of this grant is that the student must sign the TEACH Grant Agreement to Serve form. The student must also teach for four complete academic years within eight years of completing the degree.

The one problem with this grant is that if the student does not complete the service obligation, all the TEACH funds will be converted to a direct unsubsidized loan and will need to be repaid.

Military Benefits

Before I start this section, I want to thank our veterans and their families for their service. This area of the financial aid process is extremely complicated because it is highly variable; benefits change depending on your service level. In addition, military benefits can be transferred to other family members.

Follow the normal financial aid process, including completing the FAFSA to determine your financial need. Once need has been established, a financial award can be developed using the normal financial aid benefits. The financial aid process considers your military benefits and may reduce your need-based aid. This is the one disadvantage: in most cases, aid packages cannot be stacked.

Each branch of the service by geographic area has an education benefit expert. I would recommend you contact that person if you qualify for military education benefits.

Insider Note:

Listed below is a website for parents and students of military veterans that may be helpful:

https://www.vets.gov/gi-bill-comparison-tool

To maximize your benefits, you will need to have a good understanding of how your service benefits will affect your financial aid position. The college financial aid offices will also be helpful in determining this.

For students considering the military, the military academies and ROTC programs are another way of reducing your cost of college. With these options come additional commitments that should be considered before making a decision.

An example of one of the military benefits is the Iraq and Afghanistan Grant Program. This is a grant funded by the federal government and requires certain eligibility criteria set by the US Department of Education. It is provided to children who have lost a parent or guardian as a result of military service in Iraq or Afghanistan after the events of 9/11. The student must have completed the FAFSA form, be less than twenty-four years old, and be enrolled in college or career school at least part time. To be eligible for this grant, students would have an EFC that makes them ineligible for the Pell grant. The maximum award amount of this grant is the same as the Pell grant amount. This grant amount is dependent on the availability of funds, which means even if you are eligible; you may not receive the grant. Please check with your school if you think you may be eligible for this grant.

Federal Work-Study

In the need-based work-study program, students receive funds through a part-time job used to help finance tuition. Wages are usually hourly and often students need to find the job. The student's salary does not count as part of the student's income on the EFC calculation.

This financial aid is paid to the student and is not a reduction of the direct cost of the college. The wages are helpful to offset the cost of books, personal and travel expenses incurred by the student.

College Grants

Colleges have their own money to distribute to students they want to attract. This area of the financial award process can get confusing since the colleges' terminology can vary greatly. Some schools will call their grant money or need-based aid *scholarships*. When you are evaluating your financial aid awards, you need to know the difference, since these amounts can change year to year depending on your EFC and need.

College grant money is distributed by the college. I have mentioned the concept of preferential packaging used by the colleges. This is where a college tries to attract a certain type of student. This can also change by year depending on the college's admission goals.

College grant money is free money and does not need to be paid back unless the school determined it was distributed to the student using false financial information. Highly endowed colleges are able to better assist families, but getting accepted to those institutions is more difficult.

Insider Note:

Our four-year analysis process includes schools' historical gifting percentages. With this information, our clients are able to project the financial aid award and financial outcome by college. This analysis creates a customized solution based on your personal budget. It also allows the family to identify possible award letter appeal opportunities.

Analyze All of the Financing Options

Many families finance a portion of college tuition over their four years of paying for college. One of the reasons that college loans can be so confusing is there are many loans options. Each of the options have different names and terms. By the time the student graduates from college, the borrower will most likely have many types of loans from different lenders, and each loan will have its own interest rate, fees, and terms.

Let's see an example of why this financing is so complex. Listed below is an example of a possible financing decision an entering freshman may have selected. It includes the loans that are from the government and outside sources.

- Subsidized Direct (Stafford) loan $3,500

- Unsubsidized Direct (Stafford) loan $2,000

- Private loan $5,000

- Parent PLUS loan $3,000

If this is a possible list of loans for the first year of college, just imagine what this would look like after four years of education. This list could be even worse if the student is in school for a longer period of time or goes on to postgraduate studies; you could easily have sixteen different loans with different amounts and different rates by graduation time.

Why does this complexity and confusion occur? One of the reasons for the complexity is that each year new loans are established. Many of the loans are dependent on the student's FAFSA submission and the financial situation of the family.

In the sample of possible loans listed above, we also see a few different things from a legal standpoint. Some of the loans are the direct responsibility of the student and only the student. As an example, the Direct (Stafford) is the responsibility of the student. The private loan is also the responsibility of the student, but it requires a cosigner—typically the parent. If the student does not make the payment, the cosigner can be held responsible for the loan. The Parent PLUS loan is the legal responsibility of the parent who signs the note. This may be the parent's legal responsibility, but I have had clients take out this type of loan with the expectation that their child will pay it back. It is important to point out that if the child decides not to pay back the Parent PLUS loan, the parent will be held accountable.

Understanding the legal responsibility of each loan type, loan repayment and forgiveness options are all critical decisions that are not always discussed in the decision process. Proper planning is critical.

> **Insider Note:**
>
> **Failure to repay a student loan can have significant consequences. The government or lenders can garnish wages, tax refunds, and Social Security payments if the loans are not repaid.**

Listed and described below are examples of loans that are available to the student or parent:

Perkins Loan (Discontinued for New Students starting 7/2016)

A Perkins loan is a federal subsidized loan that is awarded to undergraduate students. The criteria are based on the student's financial need and certain income levels. The interest on this loan is paid by the government while the student is in school, and repayment usually begins nine months after the student graduates or drops below half-time enrollment. Please visit the US Department of Education's Federal Student Aid website for more information on Perkins loan limits. Currently, the maximum Perkins loan amount is $5,500 per year.

This program was discontinued for new students. College students who had received it for two years are eligible.

Federal Direct Subsidized Loan (Stafford)

Federal direct subsidized loans are offered by the federal government to help students pay for an associated degree, undergraduate degree, or community college, trade, career, or technical school program. The loans are based on the student's financial need, and the amount you receive cannot exceed your financial need. The US Department of Education will pay the interest on a direct subsidized loan while you are in college, and repayment will begin six months after you leave school. Loans issued after July 1, 2012, will begin charging interest one month after you graduate or stop going to school.

This loan was formerly called a subsidized Stafford loan. The new direct subsidized loan has a fixed interest rate that will change on July 1 of each year. The interest rate is fixed for the life of each loan. The rate will change if the loan is consolidated.

This loan will maintain its interest-free status while the student is in school, including undergraduate and graduate studies. To qualify for this loan, the student must complete a FAFSA form based on tax-filing status. There are overall loan limits based on the student's academic level and academic school year. The school determines your qualifications for this loan based on federal regulations.

Federal Direct Unsubsidized Loan (Stafford)

Federal direct unsubsidized loans are offered by the government to help students pay for associate and undergraduate degrees and community college, trade, career, and technical school programs. The loans are not based on the student's financial need. To qualify for this loan type, you only need to submit a FAFSA form. The interest on a direct unsubsidized loan will be charged while you are in college, and repayment will begin six months after you leave school. You can begin repayment sooner.

This loan was formerly called an unsubsidized Stafford loan. The new direct unsubsidized loan has a fixed interest rate that will change on July 1 of each year. This rate will be applied to the new amounts distributed after July 1 through June 30 of each year. The interest rate is fixed for the life of each loan. The interest rate will only change if the loan is consolidated.

This loan will always be charged interest, but you can defer payment while you are enrolled in a qualified program, including undergraduate and graduate studies. To qualify for this loan, the student must complete a FAFSA form based on tax-filing status. There are overall loan limits determined by the student's academic level and academic school year. The school determines your qualification for this loan based on federal regulations.

> **Insider Note:**
>
> All federal direct student loans, including the Perkins, are the legal responsibility of the student. Federal loans have better repayment and forgiveness options than Parent PLUS and private loans.

Federal Student Loan Limit Chart

Undergraduate (Annual)

Type/Academic Level	Subsidized	Dependent Unsubsidized	Independent Unsubsidized	Annual Limit (Dep/Indep)
Perkins	5,500			5,500
Direct First Year	3,500	2,000	4,000	5,500/7,500
Direct Second Year	4,500	2,000	4,000	6,500/8,500
Direct Third Year and Beyond for Undergrad only	5,500	2,000	4,000	7,500/9,500

Graduate (Annual)

Type/Academic Level	Subsidized	Dependent Unsubsidized	Independent Unsubsidized	Annual Limit
Direct Limit			20,500	20,500
Medical Students			40,500	40,500

Lifetime Undergraduate & Graduate Limits

Type/Academic Level	Subsidized	Dependent Unsubsidized	Independent Unsubsidized	Lifetime Limit
Perkins				27,500
Direct Federal Limit	23,000	8,000	34,000	138,500
Medical Students				224,000

Parent Direct PLUS Loans

Parent Direct PLUS loans are unsubsidized loans funded through the federal government and given to parents of dependent students to pay for college. There is interest charged to this loan while the student is in school, and the parent is responsible for repayment.

These loans are not based on the student's financial need. To qualify for this loan type, you only need to submit a FAFSA form.

The new Direct PLUS loan has a fixed interest rate that will change on July 1 of each year. The interest rate is fixed for the life of each loan. The rate will change if the loan is consolidated.

This loan will always be charged interest, but payment can be deferred while the student is enrolled in a qualified program, including undergraduate and graduate studies. To qualify for this loan, the student and parent must complete a FAFSA form based on tax-filing status. There are overall loan limits based on the student's financial aid award. The school determines your qualification for this loan based on federal regulations.

> **Insider Note:**
>
> **If the parent is denied a Parent PLUS loan, the dependent student will qualify for the loan limit of an independent student for that year. This could add an additional $4,000 or $5,000 of unsubsidized loans to the student's award.**

Graduate PLUS Loans

A Graduate PLUS loan is a federal student loan that is offered to graduate and professional students. To obtain this loan, a student must file the FAFSA to qualify, but it is not dependent on demonstrated need. The student borrower will have to have exhausted federal Stafford loan eligibility and also have passed the credit check. The loan interest can be deferred while the student is in school, and a cosigner is not required. This loan has the advantage of the borrower being able to borrow up to the total cost of education. This includes tuition, fees, room and board, books, supplies, and miscellaneous expenses minus any aid received.

Private Loan

A private student loan is obtained through a bank or other financial institution. These loans are normally limited by some approval from the college. A private student loan is limited to the cost of attendance less any financial aid the student has received. The student can take the loan out in his or her name, but it usually requires a cosigner in case of default. The interest rate is based on the borrower's and/or cosigner's credit rating. The interest rates are variable and generally near the federal Plus loan interest rate. Private loans do not have the same repayment or loan forgiveness options as the federal government loans.

The cosigner needs to understand the financial risk associated with signing for these loans. I recommend parents take out a life insurance and disability policy for the student with these types of loans. Some private loans do offer a cosigner release after some period of on-time repayment. The cosigner must ask for this release, and it is not guaranteed.

> **Insider Note:**
>
> A cosigner is the individual who signs the promissory note for a loan and is responsible for the loan if the borrower defaults.

Alternative Funding Sources

In addition to the typical educational financing options, there are other funding solutions to consider. As with any financing decision, you need to understand the risks and benefits of each option. This area of the college-funding decision cannot be answered by the college financial aid offices. These options fall into an area of personal financial planning that legally they cannot address.

Home Equity Loan or Line of Credit

This is a loan in the parent's name. There are two major advantages to this type of loan. Currently interest rates are at record low rates. These rates can be significantly lower than for Parent PLUS and private loans. As an example, when you add the fees to the Parent PLUS, the effective interest rate is over 9.0 percent if you include the administrative fees. If you have equity in your home and good credit, your home equity loan could have a rate closer to 4.25 percent. That will make the monthly repayment significantly lower.

The other advantage to the home equity loan is the interest could be deductible for some higher-income families, whereas with the federal loan it may not.

With this type of loan, the rates are often variable, which may reduce the attractiveness of these types of loans.

Home Refinancing

This loan option is similar to the home equity loan. The difference is that you may take out more money to make it available for college payments. The one problem is that once you take the extra money out, it becomes a countable asset in both financial aid calculations, whereas your home equity is not counted in the federal methodology.

Due to current interest rates, this option can be attractive, but you need to review your numbers, as with the home equity loan.

Insider Note:

Your tax advisor should review some of these alternative financing options. Each person's situation is unique and may require additional analysis to compare advantages and disadvantages of the options.

Retirement Plan Loans

For some parents taking a loan from their company retirement account is another possible source of money. You really need to be careful with this option. One of the first concerns is that it may limit your employment flexibility. Once you have a loan against your company retirement account, if you should leave or get laid off, you have sixty days to repay that loan. If you do not repay the amount, it is reported as taxable income, which raises your EFC the following year.

To use this option, you need to review your current retirement-funding plan. I talked about creating a timeline when developing your college-funding strategy. By creating a timeline, you can see how much time you have to recover after the last child has finished college.

You also need to compare the cost of borrowing money from the plan. Determine what interest rate will be used and if there are additional fees.

Retirement Contributions

In the EFC calculation, I describe how contributions to any deferred compensation plan (such as a 401k, 403b, or IRA) will be added back to your income for financial aid purposes. This can also be a source of cash flow by reducing your contribution while your children are in college.

You need to review a few things before you make this decision. You should never reduce your contribution below the company-matched rate. The company match is free money. Review the effect this decision would have on your personal retirement goals. If you are not on track or do not have sufficient recovery time after your last child finishes college, you may need to rethink the amount that can be spent or borrowed for college.

Private Scholarships

Many people have asked me where they can get scholarship money. Most scholarships are within the college's control and either come as money from endowments or just a discounted rate on tuition. There are also private scholarships available, but they require some additional work.

Most private scholarships will require submission of an application and essay. In some cases, the CSS Profile will be required, since these scholarships are based on need. To maximize this potential source of funding, investigate ideas starting with your family or local community (e.g., professional organizations that a parent or grandparent belongs to or your local bank). In most cases there will be less competition for these scholarships, meaning you have a better chance of getting the money.

Private scholarships are considered outside resources, and the scholarship money is typically sent to the college directly. This means that the college may reduce your financial aid award dollar for dollar. Depending on the college, if the scholarship plus your need-based financial aid does not exceed your need amount, the scholarship will not result in a reduction in aid. In other words, if the private scholarship is less than your financial aid gap, you are fine.

If you do not qualify for need-based aid, the private scholarship will represent a dollar-for-dollar reduction of your tuition, which is a good thing.

Other Outside Resources

Other family members or friends may consider helping a child pay for college. Before this can occur, you need to know if you qualify for need-based aid. If money is sent to the school directly and you qualify for need-based financial aid, you may want to consider a different method of receiving the funds.

The most common situation is when a grandparent sends money to a college directly, often as part of an advance estate-planning strategy (payments to a college for tuition fees can exceed the gift tax limits). If your child qualifies for need-based financial aid, this amount will typically reduce your aid dollar for dollar.

This is where some advanced planning needs to happen. If you understand your timing and EFC, a better utilization of the outside resources will maximize this money. Due to various college selections and financial strength of each family, an all in one solution for grandparents is not often available.

Company Tuition Plans

Money from tuition reimbursement programs, commonly offered to employees of colleges and universities, will sometimes be considered an outside resource by colleges. This company benefit could reduce your need-based financial aid dollar for dollar.

Many colleges offer some sort of tuition assistance for parents of the dependents or the students themselves. Recently many of these programs have seen reductions. If you have multiple children going to college, make sure you fully understand this benefit.

If your institution limits the number of semesters you will be able to receive these funds, you will need to do some additional planning. It is wise not to use this benefit for the semesters when you will qualify for the greatest amount of financial aid. This would be when your EFC is the lowest. When your EFC is the highest, using these plans would maximize their benefits.

Tax Scholarships

Taxes are one of the most overlooked areas in paying for college and can be a great source of hidden money. I am not a CPA; you need to review this information with your tax expert before you implement it. However, some tax experts may not know all of these strategies since they involve not just taxes but also the financial aid process and education-funding investments. This is especially true in situations where parents are divorced and in the area of student-loan repayment. You will need to run various scenarios for each tax situation to make the best decisions. Some situations may increase your tax bill but will be offset by a higher gain in financial aid.

Another problem many face is the planning aspect of tax strategies. Due to the timing of the tax submission to an accountant, some benefits may be forfeited since the adjustments need to be completed prior to 12/31 of the prior year and that is no longer possible. If you have a tax advisor, you may want to consider some advance planning that needs to be done prior to the fall term of a student's sophomore high school year.

An important part of utilizing the tax code is determining the sequence in which the tuition is paid, especially if you have money in a 529 plan or other college saving vehicles. By paying the college tuition a certain way, you can save thousands of dollars per year.

The first thing you need to remember is that the same qualified educational expense cannot be used multiple times for different tax advantages. As an example, you cannot pay the entire tuition with 529 money and then reuse the same tuition dollars for the American Opportunity Credit. This is where the sequence of how you pay and with what money becomes important.

To properly utilize this cost-saving strategy, you need to know your adjusted gross income (AGI) and your tax-filing status. The tax rules are very specific and confusing, and each of the tax savings has a specific income limit based on how your taxes are filed. The other confusing part of this area is that the tax year and school year do not match.

American Opportunity Credit

This is a relatively new credit, but it has the biggest advantage for joint-filing families with up to $180,000 in income and for single or head-of-household filers with income up to $90,000. To maximize this benefit, you need to pay the first $4,000 of tuition, fees, and books with cash or borrowed money. You cannot use college savings account money, such as a 529 plan or Coverdell money.

This credit is worth a maximum of $2,500 in actual money. A credit is a dollar-for-dollar reduction of your tax bill. An income tax deduction is a reduction of only taxable income and not the actual tax amount. A credit is normally a better value depending on your tax situation.

Under current law, the American Opportunity credit no longer has an expiration date. This benefit is available to each dependent undergraduate student within a family. Families with multiple children in college will qualify for this benefit. This benefit is only good for the first four years of a college education.

Lifetime Learning Credit

This benefit is similar to the American Opportunity Credit and has been around longer. The income limits are significantly lower than those of the Opportunity Credit, and these may change each year. The credit value is $2,000. You must spend $10,000 to receive the full benefit.

The advantage to this credit is that it does not need to be for the first four years of an education. It is also more restrictive, since it only includes tuition and related fees. It is also available graduate school students.

Student Loan Interest Deduction

Student-loan interest may be deductible from income tax (reducing your taxable income) depending on your income level. The income limits are set each year based on your filing status. The amount of the deduction is $2,500.

Gifting of Appreciated Assets

For families who do not qualify for need-based financial aid and have a taxable portfolio, this option can be an advantage. It is a more advanced strategy and will require some additional planning. To take advantage of this opportunity, you will need to be aware of the "kiddie tax" rules and have a brokerage account set up in the student's name and social security number.

In this situation you will transfer appreciated assets into the student's name and account. The student will then liquidate the holding and recognize the gain in his or her name and tax bracket. To avoid the "kiddie tax" rule, the total gain cannot exceed $2,100 (2016 limit). If properly used, this is similar to having a built-in 529 plan with increased investment flexibility.

This can also be part of a gifting strategy from a grandparent or other family member, but it only applies to situations where the student does not qualify for need-based financial aid.

Self-Employed Advantages

If you are self-employed, there are a few other advantages you could consider. You will need to get detailed tax advice to properly implement these recommendations. These situations are maximized with high-income families who do not qualify for need-based aid.

Bringing your child on as an employee can shift income to the child at a lower tax bracket than your own. The student will need to be a real employee and do real work to properly utilize this advantage. In addition, you could then establish a tuition-reimbursement plan. This would provide an additional $5,250 of business expense to the company.

As with other company benefits, this plan will need to be available to the other employees. You will need to evaluate this cost saving before you implement it. This benefit cannot be used by a family member until age twenty-one.

529 Money and Coverdell Saving Plans (Educational Saving Plans)

Proper use of this money can be confusing when you consider how to structure your debt and some of the tax strategies. A cost-saving opportunity that is often overlooked is the use of the 529 plans while in college. This is where knowing the state's 529 rules are important. Some states offer state income tax deductions for contributions put into a 529 plan. Most people think that 529 plans are only precollege saving options, but that is untrue.

The other issue many face is the different definitions of qualified expenses with the various tax strategies. The educational saving accounts have the broadest use. They include tuition, fees, books, room, board, and some supplies. A computer is now considered a qualified expense if the primary use is for education. In the other tax benefits, the term "qualified expenses" is used but is unique to each benefit.

Off-campus living is included as a reimbursable expense for the 529 money. You need to validate the allowable expense for off-campus living with the college, and then you will be limited to that amount of reimbursement or the amount spent, whichever is less.

The Award Letter

Appealing Your Award Letter

Many families look for help with the college award letter. Since the colleges do not disclose their process it is difficult to determine if you received all that was available. I did state earlier that the process was restrictive. This does apply to the federal rules but not the college's funds.

Appealing the financial aid letter can be a formal or informal process depending on the college. I recommend that you call the school's financial aid office to verify which process the school uses. Since award letters are not standardized, evaluating and comparing each school's award letter can be difficult. The calculation of federal financial aid is very structured, but the college's financial aid policy can be subjective.

In my opinion it's best to keep the appeal letter short and to the point; think of the reader of these appeal letters on the college side of the table. They may need to review hundreds of these letters. There has been an increased amount of press regarding the ability to negotiate with colleges, and to a certain extent, this is possible. Providing detailed information justifying your appeal will normally get you a better result. This would include two to three short sentences per item with a dollar amount associated with each item.

As I stated earlier, each year can vary based on the college acceptance yield. It never hurts to ask, but significant changes in the financial award letter are unlikely. The only exemption to that statement is if you have had a significant change in your financial situation. Events like a loss of job or income, death, and disability are reasons to contact the financial aid offices. In these situations, the college can be very understanding.

The other advice I give to my clients is to include the dollar amount of the impact for the reader. As an example, state you lost your job and your income is lowered by $30,000 in your new job. Many factors go into being accepted and the amount of financial aid you receive. Helping the appeal reader with the amount of the adjustment you need is helpful. You will need proper documentation for verification. With the example above, a recent paystub may be required for verification if the appeal is accepted.

REPAYING YOUR STUDENT LOANS THE BEST WAY

Understanding when you need to start paying back your loans is an important part of the repayment process. Repayment begins at different times, and this is why it is confusing. The loan repayment will depend on the type of loan and what year the loan was awarded to the student. In many cases, students and families decide to defer payment until after graduation. With the exceptions of Perkins and subsidized direct (Stafford) loans, interest will be charged to the loan starting sixty days after it has been dispersed.

Insider Note:

Under the student-loan repayment process, a student only gets one six-month grace period deferment. If you have used your one-time grace period, loan repayment will begin immediately.

Students and families have the option to begin payments while the student is in school. This will decrease the amount of interest and loans outstanding at graduation.

Students can use their six-month grace period if they stop going to school or take a leave of absence. When the student returns to college or a qualified program, the deferment process can be reestablished. If the student does not return to a qualified program, the payments will begin after the six-month grace period expires. Contacting your school and loan services is recommended to review all of your options.

One big change for student loans issued after July 1, 2012, concerns the interest charges. Interest will now be charged to the loan in the first month after graduation or when the student stops going to school. With older subsidized loans, there was a six-month grace period on the interest charged on the loans. That benefit is not available for the newer student loans.

The current method requires the student to participate in an exit process, normally an online video and quiz. The exit process serves to inform and educate the student about the loan amounts, the responsibility to repay the loans, and the various methods of repayment. The problem for students who decide not to continue and complete their education is that this information is normally not required or given. The EFC PLUS website has a series of videos and other information on the entire repayment process that you may find helpful.

Many schools provide some additional support, but students do not take full advantage of these programs. The other problem is that advice given by schools and loan services is often short term and focuses primarily on the monthly payment amount, with the objective of preventing students from defaulting on payments, which is critical. However, this advice does not include other personal financial decisions. Other life events normally occur just after college, including marriage and purchasing a home, and these could have a significant impact on your loan repayment decisions. This advice is not included in these programs.

Where to Begin?

Consolidating your student loans can be one of the most effective ways to avoid default issues once your repayment process starts. Before you can start a consolidation, you need to take an inventory of your student loans.

If you have delayed your consolidation and have worked for a while, additional analysis needs to be done before you consolidate your loans. With a federal loan consolidation, the time clock starts over each time you consolidate your loans. Due to this restart, if you have qualified loan repayment toward loan forgiveness you need to be careful before consolidating certain loans. By consolidating your loans, all prior payment credits to loan forgiveness will be forfeited.

Financing your college education is different from any other financing experience you are likely to have in your lifetime. The process can be very complex and confusing; this is a reason why people should consider consolidating their loans. If you have multiple loans, it may also seem like you are making a student-loan payment every week. This can be overwhelming, and it increases the risk of missing a payment. A missed payment could affect your credit and other aspects of your financial life.

What is unique about the student-loan process is not the lender but the types of loans you have. Many current student-loan holders have different loans from the same lender. To properly consolidate your loans, you need to focus on the loan type. Each loan needs to be classified as a federal or private loan, first. The lender or servicer of the loan is the next item to be identified.

For most personal loans, you typically need to contact one lender to understand your repayment options. The student-loan repayment process is not that easy, unless you consolidate your loans. Recently the federal government centralized the student-loan-servicing business, and this will make it easier in the future.

You are unable to consolidate federal and private loans together under the federal loan process; this can only be done through a private lending company. The federal loans have some advantages that are not available through private lenders, including increased repayment plans and loan forgiveness. You would forfeit these federal loan advantages by consolidating them with private loans. In most cases, I would not forfeit the federal loan benefits.

There are two major locations where student-loan data resides. For the federal loans, the data resides in a system called the National Student Loan Data System (www.NSLDS.ed.gov). To get access to the system, you will need to provide your FSA ID name and password. The second resource is your credit report. This should list all of your outstanding loans, both private and federal. You are eligible for a free annual copy of your credit report each year.

By using both sources of information, you should be able to create a complete inventory of all your student loans.

By consolidating your loans, you reduce the risk of missing payments, and you can also receive some incentives, including a .25 percent reduction for electronic withdrawal payments. It will also help you maintain good credit, which will be important in the future if you want to purchase a home or car.

Many young adults are unaware of the importance of maintaining a good credit score, also called your FICO score. This score is similar to your academic grades. Just like your academic abilities gave you options to attend various colleges, your credit score will determine the possible interest rates and amount of money that a specific lender will give you. A good credit score will show the banks or lending institutions that you are a good risk. This initial review is done with most financed purchases, except for student loans.

Insider Note:

With unconsolidated loans, you may be paying a higher monthly amount due to the default repayment method of ten years used by each servicer. By consolidating your loans, you and the single servicer can decide on a longer term, which will lower your monthly payment.

Older Loans Have Additional Issues

Due to recent changes in college lending, many students do not understand how this complexity was created. Prior to 2010, colleges had the opportunity to participate in a different student-loan program called Federal Family Education Loan (FFEL) program. The FFEL program was established as part of the Education Act of 1965. The goal of this program was to help students access funds at a private level with the government guaranteeing a certain level of interest. At the same time, the government had a direct lending program. Colleges had the option to enroll in either program.

In 2007 a national financial aid and lending scandal hit many different colleges. As a result of this scandal, many schools changed their lending policies to ensure a more transparent process. The federal government also became more involved, and decided to eliminate the FFEL program. This decision eliminated private institution in the federal student loan business.

Starting in July 2010, all colleges needed to convert to the direct lending program. These private lenders could still supply private student loans but not federal student loans. Students who attended college prior to 2010 may have federal student loans from the various lenders under the FFEL program.

With this conversion, all students starting college after July 2010 will only have direct federal loans, although they may have different types of federal loans based on their financial aid packages. The process should become easier for future students, especially in the repayment area.

As of January 1, 2014, there are four major loan servicers that are used for any new federal direct student-loan consolidation: Fed Loan Servicing (formerly AES), Great Lake, Nelnet, and Navient (formerly Sallie Mae). Fed Loan Servicing (AES) is the servicer who handles the Public Service Loan Forgiveness program. If you consolidate your federal loans, you will need to select one of the loan servicers. The old FFEL loans can still be serviced by the original servicers until you consolidate or the servicer sells your loan.

The Department of Education (DOE) has added some additional servicers to provide support to specific loan borrowers. In addition, the DOE is currently developing a more customer friendly and centralized process that will be available later in 2016.

If parents used Parent PLUS loans to finance a student's education, these loans will not appear on the student's loan inventory. They are separate loans under the parent's name. These loans have a high interest rate and different repayment options than the student loans. From a legal standpoint, the Parent PLUS loans are parents' loans and not the student's financial responsibility.

> **Insider Note:**
>
> **Parent PLUS loans are the legal responsibility of the parent. Parents need to realize that if they default on these loans, their tax refunds, wages, and Social Security payments can be partially garnished. This is becoming a growing issue for more parents.**

As you start to repay your loans, you may not realize that you are paying back a mixture of federal loans and private loans to the same lender. This is a common occurrence due to the prior student-loan environment. As you go through consolidation, you will need to separate the federal loans from the private loans to properly improve your repayment process.

For many college graduates, the monthly payment amount is shocking. Even though each year students must approve the amount of money they borrowed through the financial aid process, still many families and students do not realize the consequences of their decisions. Students often become overwhelmed at graduation when they realize the amount that was borrowed. This is why we developed our four-year cash-flow model. It reduces this risk and helps families better understand the financial commitment they are making today and in the future.

Listed below are the federal student loans that are eligible for consolidation:

- Direct subsidized loans

- Direct unsubsidized loans

- Subsidized federal Stafford loans

- Unsubsidized federal Stafford loans

- Direct PLUS loans

- PLUS loans from the Federal Family Education Loan (FFEL) program

- Supplemental loans for students (SLS)

- Federal Perkins loans

- Federal nursing loans

- Health education assistance loans

- Some existing consolidation loans

Insider Note:

The federal student loan rates change every July. Some older loans have variable rates. Depending on the direction of the interest rates, a borrower may want to accelerate or delay their consolidation.

Perkins Loan Consolidation

If you have Perkins loans in your student loan inventory, you may need to evaluate the consolidation of these loans with your other student loans. Perkins loans have some additional loan repayment advantages similar to subsidized loans. If you consolidate your Perkins loans, they convert to an unsubsidized loan within the consolidation, resulting in the loss of these additional benefits.

Your best option is not to consolidate the Perkins loans if you are planning to return to college later because interest is not charged on Perkins and subsidized loans while in school.

Loan Repayment Options

In the chapter covering student loans, I explained the various loans that are available to students and parents for funding education. Another area of college affordability is planning how repayment can help you afford the education you want. By understanding the various rules of repayment and loan forgiveness, your debt repayment can be manageable and not a surprise.

There are currently nine different federal student loan repayment methods. Depending on the type of student-loans, income level, marital status, and a few other key points, making the correct choice can be difficult. Listed below are the current federal student loan repayment methods:

Standard Ten-Year Repayment Plan

The loan payment is a fixed amount and is paid off in ten years. This method can be used for all federal student loans and is the normal, default repayment method. This number is important to know, since this is the highest amount you can pay if you use any of the income-determined methods. If you no longer qualify for the income-determined methods, but still qualify for the Public Service Loan Forgiveness program, this will be the amount you will need to pay.

Pro: Lowest total loan repayment cost and shortest period repayment method.

              This method qualifies for the Public Service Loan Forgiveness programs (PSLF).

Con: Payment will be the highest flat amount when compared to the other loan repayment plans.

Graduated Repayment Plan

The repayment amount is lower at first, and then it increases every two years. Payment is finished in ten years. This method is affordable at the beginning but can get very expensive in the later years.

Pro: Lower payment initially.

Con: You will pay more interest over ten years than with the standard repayment plan.

              Interest accrues at the beginning of the payment schedule.

              It does not qualify for the PSLF program.

              Payments can get expensive in the later years of the loan.

Extended Repayment Plan

The repayment amount is fixed for the life of the repayment. The number of years of extension is based on the outstanding loan balance. This can be an attractive method for cash-flow reasons, and, if combined with a prepayment plan, it can help you avoid default.

Pro: Monthly payment will be lower than the ten-year standard repayment plan.

              It can be extended for twenty-five years.

              It will give you the lowest fixed payment without the risk of your loan balance increasing.

              It is a valid method for Parent PLUS loans.

Con: It is the most expensive repayment total over the life of the loan.

It is not a valid repayment plan for the PSLF program.

> **Insider Note:**
>
> The extended repayment method is sometimes called the standard method on some government websites. When using the income-determined repayment methods, the highest amount that you can pay is also called the standard method. This is in reference to the standard ten-year payment and not the extended repayment described above. Understanding the difference in terms is especially critical when the PSLF program is being utilized.

Extended Graduated Repayment Plan

The repayment amount will increase in cost every two years, which is considered to be semifixed. The number of years of extension is based on the outstanding loan balance. This can be an attractive method for cash-flow reasons, but it can get very expensive in the later years.

Pro: Monthly payment will be lower than with the ten-year standard repayment plan.

It can be extended for twenty-five years.

Con: This is one of the most expensive methods of repayment over the life of the loan.

It is not a valid repayment plan for the PSLF program.

Income-Based Repayment (IBR)

This repayment plan is based on your income, the national poverty level index, and family size. The monthly payment is limited to 15 percent of your discretionary income. *Discretionary income* is the difference between your adjusted gross income and 150 percent of the poverty guidelines for your family size and the state you reside in. This method of repayment is not applicable to Parent PLUS loans.

Pro: It qualifies for the PSLF program (ten years).

The debt is forgiven after twenty-five years.

Helps students stay current on loans when their income is low.

It is an alternative to deferment.

Unpaid subsidized loan interest is paid by the government for the first three years on a prorated basis.

Con: Loan balance could go up if using this method (negative amortization).

Need to apply each year based on current income or prior year's tax-return AGI.

Once a person is married, both incomes will be included if filing married and joint.

Loan forgiveness after twenty-five years is taxable, excluding PSLF program.

Insider Note:

Negative amortization can occur when the payment on the student loan is less than the interest that accrues each month. This causes the balance on the loan to increase.

Pay As You Earn (PAYE)

This loan repayment method is based on the student's adjusted gross income and is the newest income-determined method of repayment. The monthly payment under PAYE is calculated at 10 percent of your discretionary income. To be eligible for PAYE, the person must have no federal student loan debt balance prior to October 1, 2007, and have received a federal student loan program distribution after October 1, 2011. It can be used for all student direct loans, excluding direct student consolidated loans that include a Parent PLUS loan within them. This method of repayment is not available for Parent PLUS loans.

Pro: Lowest possible payment if disposable income is low.

    After twenty years of repayment, any outstanding balance is forgiven.

    It qualifies for the Public Service Loan Forgiveness program.

    It is an alternative to deferment.

    The government for the first three years on a prorated basis pays a portion of the subsidized loan interest charges.

Con: Unpaid interest is accrued during repayment and can have negative amortization limited to 10 percent of the original balance.

    Need to apply each year based on current income or prior year's tax-return AGI.

    Once a person is married, both incomes will be included if filing married and joint.

    Loan forgiveness after twenty years is taxable, excluding PSLF program.

Revised Pay As You Earn (REPAYE)

REPAYE is the newest of the income-driven repayment methods. It became available in mid-December, 2015. The REPAYE is an extension of the current Pay AS Your Earn (PAYE) program. The development of this new Income Driven Method is part of the commitment of the Obama Administration to help protect college borrowers and prevent student loan default.

The REPAYE method includes a larger number of borrowers who have federal student loans. PAYE repayment method is only available for newer borrowers. Under the PAYE, participating students cannot have a federal loan debt balance prior to October 1, 2007 and need to have recent loans after October 1, 2011. REPAYE is not dependent on these specific dates for a borrower to be eligible to use this method.

REPAYE caps the monthly student loan payment amount to 10 percent of their annual adjusted income allocated on a monthly basis. For borrower who did not qualify for PAYE due to the debt timing this is a significant advantage. As default rates continue to rise, the new REPAYE method can help borrowers stay current with their repayments and reduce the financial stress on their budget.

Pro   No loan origination date limit
                Qualifies for Public Service Loan Forgiveness
                It is an alternative to deferment

Con   If married, both incomes will be included. Tax filing status is excluded for married couples under this process.
Unpaid interest is accrued during repayment and can have a negative amortization limited to 10 percent of the original balance
Need to apply each year based on based on current income or prior year's AGI. Married couples cannot separate their pay under this method.
Loan Forgiveness is available for undergraduate debt after 20 year and 25 years for post-graduate debt

Income-Contingent Repayment (ICR)

ICR repayment is intended to make payments more affordable. Payment is determined by your total direct loan debt as well as your adjusted gross income and family size. ICR can be used for all direct student loans. This is one of the original income-determined repayment methods.

Pro: The debt is forgiven after twenty-five years.
               Available for Parent PLUS loans if consolidated in the direct program.

It qualifies for the Public Service Loan Forgiveness program.

Con: Loan payment changes as income changes.
Minimum payment must cover loan interest charge.
PAYE and IBR are normally better solutions.
Need to apply each year based on current income or prior year's tax-return AGI.

Income-Sensitive Repayment

This repayment method is based on your annual AGI. It can be used with subsidized and unsubsidized federal Stafford loans, FFEL PLUS loans, and FFEL consolidation loans.

Pro: Loan is repaid in twenty-five years.

Con: Payment changes as your income changes.
Need to apply each year based on current income or prior year's tax-return AGI.
Minimum payment must cover loan interest charge.
Loan balance could go up if using this method (negative amortization).

Deferment and Forbearance

For some borrowers, financial hardship can occur. Deferment and forbearance are additional methods of staying current on your student loans during difficult times. These programs allow you to postpone payment for some allotted time.

With the new income-determined methods, an easier method may be to contact your servicer and move to IBR or PAYE to stay current. It's best to avoid student-loan default; the penalties are severe.

Insider Note:

The Department of Education has further information concerning the penalties of defaulting on a student loan. The website is https://studentaid.ed.gov/repay-loans/default/collections.

GETTING YOUR STUDENT LOANS FORGIVEN

One-way students and parents can deal with the increasing cost of college is through the utilization of loan forgiveness and loan repayment programs. With these programs, some or all of a borrower's debt will be forgiven if the repayment criteria are fulfilled.

Before you consider using loan forgiveness as a college-funding strategy, you need to understand the rules. Too often we hear the headlines and do not investigate the specifics of the program. The loan forgiveness programs are a perfect example. These plans offer great benefits, but complying with rules can be difficult to plan for while in college.

The loan forgiveness rules are very complex and difficult to understand. In addition many of the student-loan forgiveness programs require a minimum of five to twenty-five years to receive the full benefits. Some of the loan forgiveness programs become taxable income, which may result in an unexpected increase in taxes.

The life changes many people experience after graduation can make repayment difficult. This is a time when graduates may be getting married, purchasing a home, or buying a car. All these events affect a person's ability to pay student loans and stay within the rules of loan forgiveness. These life events also have a significant impact on graduates' lifestyle and financial decisions. Student-loan repayment needs to be a priority due to the severity of penalties and default.

Many students and families do not understand that your income, tax status, employer, consolidation, repayment, and loan forgiveness are all intertwined. As an example, only certain loans qualify for loan forgiveness, and you need to use certain repayment methods to qualify for loan forgiveness. Where you work or the company's financial structure will also limit your ability to qualify for many of the accelerated forgiveness timeframes.

The Public Service Loan Forgiveness program is a perfect example of the complexity that is often misunderstood or overlooked. Only direct federal loans under the student's name will qualify for forgiveness. You can only use the standard payment method (ten years), income-based repayment method (IBR), income-contingent repayment method (ICR), Pay as you earn repayment method (PAYE) and Revised Pay As You Earn (REPAYE) repayment method. There are other repayment methods available, but only the five listed above will qualify toward the Public Service Loan Forgiveness program.

After making 120 (ten years) on-time direct federal loan payments using the four methods listed above, you will qualify for loan forgiveness. The 120 payments do not need to be sequential. In order to qualify for loan forgiveness, you must be working full time for the government or a nonprofit organization. Be aware that some nonprofit positions do not satisfy the loan forgiveness employment requirement. It is important to check with your employer to verify your eligibility. Currently, Fed Loan Servicing handles all public service loan forgiveness clients.

Having a plan is critical. You need to understand the impact of your career decisions during the repayment period. Factors such as changing jobs, whether your company is for profit or nonprofit, and the way you file your taxes could significantly impact your student-loan forgiveness outcome and the amount you pay.

Creating a Loan Forgiveness Plan

It's important to create a plan to maximize your benefits for loan forgiveness and understand where you are in the loan forgiveness process and the financial impact of a career change.

We've discussed the importance of taking an inventory of your loans and understanding the different types of student loans. In most cases it's best to consolidate your loans under the direct federal program. This would be the first step to maximizing your potential for loan forgiveness.

Moving all of your federal loans to the direct program will qualify you for the Public Service Loan Forgiveness program if your employment fits the other criteria. There are other forgiveness programs that will forgive federal student loans that do not need to be direct student loans. These methods are primarily for people working in the areas of education and health care.

Once you start your career, talk to the human resource department at your company to get the detailed information on which options are available. You need to create a short and long-term plan. The company's human resource department may be limited in the information they can provide, but they should be able to give you information on any of the programs the employer offers. The human resource department typically will not analyze your numbers. As stated in the repayment section, creating a repayment strategy is critical. Knowing the programs that an employer offers is important in selecting the best employment option if you are considering loan forgiveness.

Loan forgiveness is limited to only five repayment methods:

- Standard repayment (ten-year only)

- Income-based repayment (IBR)

- Income-contingent repayment (ICR)

- Pay as you earn (PAYE)

- Revised Pay as you earn (REPAYE)

You can use any combination of these methods, and the method will most likely change as your income increases over time. As an example, a doctor may enter into a program using income-based repayment, but over the ten years of repayment his or her income will likely increase significantly. In this care, the doctor would no longer qualify for the IBR plan. At that point, he or she may need to switch to the standard ten-year payment method. Selecting the right repayment plan is critical for maintaining PSLF eligibility.

You need to ask yourself, what will be forgiven if I am paying back the loans, and will I be finished repaying the loans after ten years? For example, you could be paying under IBR for seven years before your income goes up and you only need to pay the ten-year standard rate for three years. The amount forgiven could still be substantial.

You can see how important planning is to maximize this option. If you properly plan and understand the rules, other financial decisions become possible. Knowing that your student loans will be forgiven at a certain age may allow you to plan on a home purchase or start a family. Loan repayment mistakes can cost you thousands of dollars and make it more difficult to achieve your other personal goals.

Loan forgiveness planning is highly dependent on your personal financial situation. Listed below are many of the issues that require consideration:

- Types of loans

- Employer

- Salary

- Tax-filing status

- Repayment method

- Type of job

Importance of Career Path

Your career path is important in the strategy for repayment. Your career decisions have a significant impact on your financial future. As an example, a nurse may have the choice to work at a nonprofit hospital or in a private doctor's office. This career decision will impact the loan forgiveness potential of that person. The nurse who works for the nonprofit hospital will qualify for loan forgiveness after 120 on-time payments while a nurse who works for a private doctor will not qualify for loan forgiveness until after twenty or twenty-five years depending on which repayment method he or she uses under current law.

Having a general understanding of your career direction will help you make better decisions about both loan forgiveness and repayment methods. As you can see with the example above, sometimes your career will dictate where you work. In other cases you may have the freedom to select where you work to maximize the various financial options regarding loan forgiveness.

An important part of this process is to confirm with your employer which programs are available to you. Some companies have additional programs that may allow you to reduce your student debt more quickly. Confirm whether the company you work for is a government agency or a nonprofit organization. A nonprofit company will typically have a tax file structured code that is called a 501c3 organization. You need to confirm the non-profit status, since many governments and nonprofits outsource various services to private industries. Working in a hospital or a government facility does not necessarily qualify your loans for loan forgiveness programs.

Good Record Keeping Is Required

To qualify for the various loan forgiveness programs, proper documentation is required. This is often overlooked; loan forgiveness is so far into the future that people don't often think about it right away. As an example, the first PSLF payment to the servicers will not be made until 2017. This process is different from any other financial process you face. While you only need to maintain tax records for seven years, for the Public Service Loan Forgiveness program, you will need to document your work history for the duration of the 120 on-time payments. This may go beyond the ten years depending on your employment.

To qualify for the program, the records you keep must prove that you were employed full time while making the payments. Your W-2 and tax forms do not validate your level of employment; they only display the amount of money you made in a specific tax year. The form that is required is called the Certification of Employment for Public Service Loan Forgiveness. This form is available on the government website and our website.

It is recommended that you have the form completed each year or each time you change jobs or positions while repaying your student loans. It is critical that you maintain this documentation along with your repayment history to properly qualify for the various forgiveness programs available. It is highly recommended that you maintain both paper and digital copies of these forms.

You may need to keep these records for longer than ten years. For example, imagine you work for a nonprofit company right out of college and then decide to work in the private sector for two or three years. After those two or three years, you decide to return to a nonprofit or government area of employment. In this case, you would need to maintain employment records for more than twelve or thirteen years in order to qualify for the forgiveness program. In addition, you will need to prove that you are a full-time employee. The employer would sign off the form or HR department as you changed each of those jobs. Only the nonprofit or government jobs would need to be documented.

Due to current economic conditions, companies or organizations you work for may not exist by the time you qualify to apply for loan forgiveness. This is where having both the form and your tax information to confirm employment is critical each year.

The discussion above has been primarily focused on the shorter-term forgiveness programs. Under current law the loan forgiveness process also forgives federal loans after twenty or twenty-five years, depending on the repayment method. These forgiveness programs do not require the same amount of documentation as listed above. You will still need to document that you have been repaying for a certain amount of time, but that is all. This additional documentation is only needed for the income-based repayment (IBR), income-contingent repayment (ICR), pay-as-you-earn (PAYE) and revised-pay-as-you-earn (REPAYE) methods. The other methods, such as standard, extended, and graduated, do not have forgiveness because the debt will be repaid within the timeframe selected.

There are a few exceptions to both the accelerated and normal forgiveness programs. Businesses that are for profit, labor unions, some political organizations, and some religious organizations do not qualify for loan forgiveness. This is another reason to verify with your employer to see if you will qualify for the accelerated loan forgiveness programs. Again, the structure of your employer is so important. I would confirm with the employer and then check with the loan servicer that the employer you are working for really does qualify. I recommend that you get that in writing from the loan servicer and keep the letter in your records.

Volunteer Services

Another great way to accelerate your repayment process is to do volunteer work through one of the national organizations. AmeriCorps, Peace Corps, and Volunteers in Service to America are all organizations that offer additional loan repayment contributions against your student debt. In addition, your service time will count toward the federal public service timeframe of 120 payments if you select the proper repayment method.

All the service organizations are dedicated to improving the communities they serve. As a benefit, you may receive some pay for the work you do and a direct payment to your student debt. These payments will only be applied to federal loans. Always check the loan forgiveness program with any organization you consider working for.

It is recommended that you consolidate or at a minimum convert all of your federal loans to the direct federal loan program. The one exception is a Perkins loan; if this is consolidated, some benefits could be lost in the acceleration of its repayment.

As stated earlier in the book, you need to make sure to document your work history. In many cases, it will be difficult to confirm volunteer work history since employees are very transient.

Many students with low-paying jobs opt to defer their loans; this is a mistake. With some of the new income-based repayment methods, it is more beneficial to consolidate your loans and begin repayment once your full-time work begins. This is especially true if you know your career will most likely be in the government or nonprofit worlds. By starting under a specific repayment method and being a full-time employee, your clock will start against your 120 on-time payments. Due to your low income, your payment will most likely be very low, if not zero.

If you use the deferment method, your volunteer service time will not count toward the 120 on-time payments. Evaluate the income-based and pay-as-you-earn student-loan repayment methods before you enter into one of these volunteer service organizations.

Teacher Programs

There is a series of additional loan forgiveness programs specifically for teachers. They vary by school district and also by the subjects taught. Many of the enhanced teacher loan forgiveness programs require the teacher to be in the classroom, so administrators and counselors typically do not qualify for these accelerated loan forgiveness programs.

Insider Note:

The American Federation of Teachers maintains a website with various loan forgiveness and grant programs available to teachers within the United States. The website is listed below: www.aft.org/yourwork/tools4teachers/fundingdatabase/.

It's important for new teachers to confirm the type of school and school district they'll be working in. Working in a Title 1 school can have significant advantages for the reduction of student debt. You need to work in that environment for five consecutive school years to qualify for these enhanced programs. Based on the subject you teach, the amount that can be forgiven can increase. As an example, math and science teachers will receive more forgiveness money than English or history teachers. You need to complete the five years, and the loan forgiveness payment is made in your sixth year teaching.

Remember to keep accurate records and get the current form for this additional program. I would recommend that you contact your school district's human resource department to confirm if your position and teaching subject qualify for teacher loan forgiveness programs.

This loan forgiveness also has a sequence of loans that are paid back first. Here again the Perkins loans have some additional benefits within the forgiveness programs, so you may not want to consolidate them into your federal direct consolidation.

Some states offer additional incentives for teachers to work in less-desirable locations. These programs may require you to relocate or work in lower-income or more demanding environments.

For some teachers there may be additional complexity with the teacher loan forgiveness programs. The loan forgiveness amount could be taxable, depending on the program. Any accelerated payment of debt is normally a good thing. If the loan forgiveness amount is taxable, it will raise your income and may affect your monthly payment the following year under the income-based repayment methods.

Attorney Loan Forgiveness

Changes in the subsidized loan program for postgraduate studies have significantly raised the cost of borrowing money for any of these programs. This is especially true for students attending law school. In 2010 subsidized Stafford loans for postgraduate studies were eliminated.

Due to the high cost of law school, this added significant interest cost to students financing their postgraduate studies.

After graduating from law school, you may still qualify for the federal Public Service Loan Forgiveness program. There are other programs offered for lawyers who serve in the public interest and similar organizations. These programs are offered by some law schools and various legal organizations.

As stated earlier some of these loan forgiveness programs can be considered income and may have an impact on your loan repayment method.

Utilizing the various income-dependent repayment methods may be the best way to initially manage your monthly debt. If you have high debt and lower income, using the income-based repayment methods could make the monthly payment manageable. If low income high college debt continues for a significant amount of time, it will become a financial burden for a significant part of your life.

If you know you will not qualify for the Public Service Loan Forgiveness program, you should consider some of the other fixed repayment methods. In most cases, the income based repayment methods are short term solutions to avoid default.

Medical Loan Forgiveness

People in the medical profession have one major advantage: many of their employers are nonprofit organizations, and the employees are paid competitive salaries. This is not the same for attorneys and other professions that require post graduate degrees. Many of the medical careers offer higher-paying jobs that are not always available in the private sector.

In addition, some areas of the country offer loan-reduction incentives to come and work there.

Another unique feature for lowering student debt for the medical professional is the way the certification process works. Some medical careers require a residency or training period while you are being paid a lower salary. This is a perfect time to begin your loan repayment using one of the income-dependent repayment methods. By utilizing this lower monthly payment, you can start your loan forgiveness payment credits.

Understanding the best ways to consolidate the loans will be important to maximize your loan forgiveness, especially if you chose to work for the government or in a nonprofit environment. Each student-loan consolidation restarts your loan payment history toward loan forgiveness under the PSLF program. If not done correctly, this could cost you money and qualified payment credits.

Tax Impact of Loan Forgiveness

Qualifying for loan forgiveness is a great way to reduce your debt level and improve your quality of life. However, there is one disadvantage to many of the loan forgiveness programs: under the IRS regulations, most debt forgiveness is considered taxable income. The amount of the loan forgiven becomes taxable income in many cases. The one exception is the Public Service Loan Forgiveness program. This shows where personal financial advice needs to be incorporated into the borrower's loan repayment planning.

As an example, your employer pays a portion of your student loans and pays the amount directly to the loan servicer. On your W2 Tax form that amount will appear and will become income. The student-loan forgiveness amount is taxable. It may affect your monthly loan payment the following year if you are using one of the income-determined methods. Some long-term personal financial planning along with your loan repayment and loan forgiveness is important.

An income increase due to a loan forgiveness payment will most likely increase your monthly payment. Your payment will be impacted for as long as you receive forgiveness payments. This is common for many of the teacher programs, since incentives are commonly paid out over multiple years. Having a long-term plan and understanding when these increases will occur is critical. Changing payment plans can have a negative impact on qualifying for the maximum loan forgiveness amounts.

Professional Advice

In the past few years, there has been a significant increase in the number of companies promoting loan consolidation and forgiveness advice. Both students and parent need to be careful. When seeking this expertise, you need to get answers beyond the lowest payment and employment requirements.

Most people make mistakes in the area of personal financial planning and how it relates to the loan repayment methods. The decisions on your personal financial side, such as tax-filing status, could have a significant impact on maximizing this benefit. You want a person who can bring together both personal finance and loan forgiveness expertise.

CREATING YOUR PLAN

This book has walked you through the college affordability process and given you insights into the complicated issues that parents and students encounter during their college journey.

Many families underestimate how dependent the financial aid process is on the family's personal finances, including decisions made prior, during, and after college. Making the best college financial decision entails the whole process of saving for, financing, and repaying education loans after graduation.

The student especially needs to understand this commitment. There are academic, emotional, and financial decisions that need to be made. Some of these decisions may not be easy. If you focus on the outcome, it will be easy to justify these choices. I want to stress the importance of open communication throughout this process. Let your child have a realistic idea of the colleges you can afford and your expectations of them while they are in college.

The increased cost of education has put significant pressure on families and students. Many of these decisions will affect both the family and the student for many years into the future. Errors can be avoided or minimized with proper college planning. By creating a four-year academic and financial plan, you can make many decisions more easily. By utilizing our college affordability videos, our EFC Plus tool and having better financial information, families will better be able to compare the value of each college. When you factor in the academic programs and campus life, you can make an informed decision.

I would like to point out again how important the graduation and retention rates of each college are in the college evaluation process. Graduating in four years and not transferring can be one of the best cost-saving strategies.

You also know now that finances are the biggest reason why students leave or transfer from a college. This again confirms how important it is for families to make the right financial decisions at the beginning of the college process.

There is an abundance of free resources available to parents and students. Be cautious when seeking financial advice. Remember, when creating a comprehensive college plan, you must disclose your entire financial position.

Listed below are the key points to focus on as you evolve through the college process from a financial standpoint. Some of these points will cross over different stages.

Precollege

- Understand your financial aid position or EFC

  o All four quadrants of the EFC

- Establish a college saving plan

  o Know your state 529 saving plan rules

- Identify career and educational requirements for career options

- Evaluate colleges on a value basis not by sticker price

- Create a four-year cash analysis

College Years
- Understand educational tax benefits that you qualify for

- Revisit state 529 plan rules

- Create four-year academic and financial plans

- Determine debt structure

    o Understand legal responsibility of the loans

    o Factor in loan repayment options and forgiveness plans

- Determine outcome of education

    o Create a personal income and expense budget for after graduation

    o Identify and discuss how career will affect quality-of-life

Post college
- Inventory student loans

- Evaluate loan repayment and forgiveness options

- Stay current on student-loan repayment

- Understand the impact of other personal decisions on student-loan repayment decisions

    o Getting married and tax-filing status

    o Loan balance on other major purchases, such as a home

I hope you have found this book helpful in making the best college decision. My approach is a little different, since I focus on how college affordability can affect your life both today and after college graduation. My goal was to help both families and students decrease any costly mistakes.

As a parent who has completed the process of educating my children, and as a financial planner, I know how difficult these decisions can be. I hope this information will alleviate some of your stress so you can enjoy this stage in your child's life. Good luck, and enjoy the ride!

INDEX

T

Tax scholarship, 91-92

Teacher Education Assistance for College and Higher Education Grant (TEACH), 78, 79

Test score-optional colleges, 12

Traditional IRA, 55

Trust Beneficiary, 57

U

Unsubsidized Direct (Stafford) loan, 82, 84, 85

Uniform Gift to Minor Account (UGMA), 51

US Saving bonds, 52

Other items

529 plans, 52

401k Plans, 39

ABOUT THE AUTHOR

Fred Amrein brings personal financial-planning expertise to the entire college financial aid process. He is the founding principal of Amrein Financial, an independent, fee-only financial firm based in Pennsylvania. Fred is also the owner and developer of EFCPLUS.com, a website that focuses on the entire college financial decision process with video library covering topics from how to save for college to student-loan forgiveness.

He has also developed, EFC PLUS, a consumer and advisor college financial planning software tool that evolves with the student and family throughout each stage of the college financial process. This would include saving for college, paying for college and student loan repayment.

Fred is a board member of the National College Advocacy Group (NCAG) and a member of the National Association of Personal Financial Advisors (NAPFA). His education includes an MBA in finance and a BS in accounting and marketing from Saint Joseph's University. He has a Charter Financial Consultant (ChFC) designation from the American College.

Other personal financial- and college-planning organizations have recognized Fred's expertise. He has been a speaker for the Independent Education Consultant Association (IECA), Higher Education Consultant

Association (HECA), American Institute for CPA (AICPA), Pennsylvania Institute for CPA (PICPA), National Association of Personal Financial Advisors (NAPFA), and National College Advocacy Group (NCAG).

Fred has been quoted in the *Wall Street Journal, BusinessWeek, Journal of Financial Planning, US News and World Report, Kiplinger,* and many other national publications. In addition, he appears on various media programs speaking about personal financial topics, mostly educational-funding and student-loan repayment issues. Fred has also developed several software programs that analyze college costs, financing options, and student-loan repayment. He is currently developing a student and parent financial literacy program addressing decisions related to college financing.

He is the father of three daughters who have all graduated from college on time. Their college experience includes two school changes, two major changes, and student athletics. Fred has been married for over thirty years.

FOOTNOTE REFERENCES

---

1. "Enrollment Rates of 18- to 24-Year-Olds in Degree-Granting Institutions, by Level of Institution and Sex and Race/Ethnicity of Student: 1967 through 2012," *Digest of Education Statistics*, accessed August 29, 2014, http://nces.ed.gov/programs/digest/d13/tables/dt13_302.60.asp.

2. Ibid.

3. "Colleges and Universities that Claim to Meet Full Financial Need," *U.S. News & World Report*, accessed August 29, 2014, http://www.usnews.com/education/best-colleges/paying-for-college/articles/2013/09/18/colleges-that-claim-to-meet-full-financial-need-2014.

4. "Parents Projected to Spend $241,080 to Raise a Child Born in 2012, According to USDA Report," US Department of Agriculture, accessed August 29, 2014, http://www.usda.gov/wps/portal/usda/usdahome?contentid=2013/08/0160.xml.

5. "Charts: Just How Fast Has College Tuition Grown?" U.S. News & World, accessed August 29, 2014, http://www.usnews.com/news/articles/2013/10/23/charts-just-how-fast-has-college-tuition-grown.

6. "Student Debt Swells, Federal Loans Now Top a Trillion," Consumer Financial Protection Bureau, accessed August 29, 2014, http://www.consumerfinance.gov/newsroom/student-debt-swells-federal-loans-now-top-a-trillion/.

Made in the USA
Middletown, DE
03 August 2016